BEAUTIFUL SCARS

BEAUTIFUL SCARS

STEELTOWN SECRETS, MOHAWK SKYWALKERS AND THE ROAD HOME

TOM WILSON

DOUBLEDAY CANADA

Doubleday Canada and colophon are registered trademarks of Penguin Random House Canada Limited

LIBRARY AND ARCHIVES CANADA CATALOGUING IN PUBLICATION

Wilson, Tom, 1959-, author
    Beautiful scars / Tom Wilson.

Issued in print and electronic formats.
ISBN 978-0-385-68565-8 (hardcover).—ISBN 978-0-385-68566-5 (EPUB)

    1. Wilson, Tom, 1959-. 2. Wilson, Tom, 1959- —Family. 3. Birthparents—Ontario—Hamilton—Identification. 4. Adopted children—Ontario—Hamilton—Biography. 5. Mohawk Indians—Ontario—Hamilton—Biography. I. Title.

HV874.82.W55A3 2017   362.734092   C2017-904461-3
                                                  C2017-904462-1

Jacket and book design: Lisa Jager
Jacket photo: © Jen Squires

Printed and bound in the USA

Published in Canada by Doubleday Canada,
a division of Penguin Random House Canada Limited

www.penguinrandomhouse.ca

10 9 8 7 6 5 4 3 2 1

Penguin
Random House
DOUBLEDAY CANADA

TO THOSE WHO HAVE COME BEFORE, THOSE THAT
WILL COME AFTER AND THOSE THAT KEEP ME GOING.

EVERY NIGHT I LOOK

FROM STAR TO STAR

THREE THOUSAND MILES THROUGH THESE EMPTY BARS

AND I END UP SLEEPING

OUT IN MY CAR

AND THE MOON SHINES OFF MY BEAUTIFUL SCARS

CONTENTS

TRUTH

SECRETS

WAKING UP—ONE

remember waking up in a wooden crib, crying. I was an infant, no more than a year old. There was a lamp, a pink lamb or elephant I think, and its low-wattage bulb filled my corner of the room. The faded walls were the grey of a 1950s institution, and were patchy, like the painter had dropped the roller and split before finishing the job. Right beside me a tall dresser was overflowing with stuffed animals, as if someone had had a lucky night playing skee-ball at a Conklin midway. Some of the animals were hand-sewn. Scrawny, confused-looking creatures, crooked eyes made from hand-me-down flannel pyjamas. Clean but worn.

I never bothered much with these stuffed toys, but my one cherished friend among them was a cloth-bodied, plastic-headed rabbit. Peter, of course. I never went anywhere without him. The story goes that Bunny, my mother, and my cousin Janie were looking out through the back-bedroom window at the snow falling when they saw Bunny's dog, Trixie, tossing something up in the air, dashing across the snow, wrestling it in her mouth and tossing it up again. The dog came in through the side door and Bunny grabbed the dirty object from her, washed it and put it in my crib. "And that, Tommy, was your first toy," Bunny used to proudly tell me.

I loved when Bunny told that story because she didn't have any other stories about me as a baby, and I remember thinking that maybe I'd been dragged in by Trixie from that same yard and pulled from her mouth by Bunny because there was no conceivable way I belonged here with these people. Even as a kid my existence as the son of Bunny and George Wilson seemed far-fetched to me. When I went over it in my head, none of it added up. The other kids on East 36th Street in Hamilton used to tell me stories of their mothers being pregnant and their newborn siblings coming home from the hospital. Nobody ever talked about Bunny's and my return from the hospital. In my mind my birth was like the nativity, only with gnarly dogs and dirty snow and a chipped picket fence and old blind people with short tempers and dim lights, ashtrays full of Export Plain cigarette butts and bottles of rum.

Once, when I was about four, I asked Bunny, "How come I don't look anything like you and George? How come you are old and the other moms are young?"

"There are secrets I know about you that I'll take to my grave," she responded. And that pretty well finished that. Bunny built up a wall to protect her secrets, and as a result I built a wall to protect myself. I tried to hide how I felt from everyone, including myself. I knew I would be judged harshly if I were to reveal what I was thinking, what I was feeling, so I just dulled the edges of my existence so no one would know who I had living inside me. I became a secret to myself.

I still have those toys, stuffed in a garbage bag tossed somewhere on the third floor of my house. They've survived dozens of moves and have stayed in that garbage bag for the better part of fifty-seven years. I come across them once in a while, usually when I'm cleaning out one area of my house and fixing up another. The bag only gets opened when someone has to check to see what's inside. My ex-wife, old girlfriends, movers and band crews have all looked down the open mouth of the green Glad bag and into my beginnings. Like Rosebud.

"Hey, do you want these? They're a bunch of old kids' toys," or "Fuck—look at this weird shit. . . . These things are scary," or "Throw them out, throw them all out. Jesus Christ, what are you keeping them for?" girlfriends have said. Over the years, I've managed to hold on to the toys but not the girlfriends. I kept the toys as a reminder of where I came from, or at least where I thought I came from. That green plastic garbage bag hung around for years to honour my first memory of feeling hollowed out. Like an outsider in my home, like a stranger not knowing what the heck was going on. The first time I felt I was in the wrong place, like a spaceship had dropped me in the wrong yard.

BUNNY WILSON'S KID

THE NEEDY

Bunny and George were older. George was fifty-one and Bunny forty-seven when I showed up in 1959. George collected a hundred dollars for working five days a week on a "blind stand." These small confectionery posts were organized by the Canadian National Institute for the Blind and were meant to provide blind vets with work and purpose. George also collected a disability pension for having had his head blown open and his eyes taken away from him as an RCAF flight sergeant.

Bunny stayed home wearing an apron and taking care of things like the washing and ironing and me. I guess she was a housewife of sorts, although the house was always very messy. Things were always kept off the floor so George could manoeuvre his way through the house, and as a result there were pathways

made throughout the living room, walled in by stacks of news-
papers and magazines and toys and ironing boards piled on
either side. The place was a disaster, but at least George would
not trip while getting to his easy chair. Bunny wasn't much of a
cook either. We lived off TV dinners, instant potatoes, wieners,
Kraft Dinner, Pop-Tarts and cans of anything she happened to
reach for and pull off the shelf—waxed beans, creamed corn,
Alpha-Getti, and on down the line. I can't remember an onion
ever hitting a saucepan. Nothing was made from scratch. Bunny
would sit in the kitchen reading the paper in her underwear
and an apron pondering her next move and telling Trixie,
"Well, I guess it's time for us to strap on the old goddamn feed
bag, isn't it."

Bunny left school at fourteen to start working at the Sun Life
building in downtown Montreal. She took the train into Montreal
every morning, got off at Windsor Station and walked with the
masses across Dorchester Square, where she reported to her desk
in the tallest building in the largest city in the Dominion of
Canada. She went straight from a one-room schoolhouse in the
sticks of Quebec to filing the foreign insurance policies of fancy
clients and answering the calls of wild and worldly customers in
faraway lands she'd only seen on maps, places like Cuba and
Caracas. She went to mass on her lunch break, and disappeared
behind secret doors in speakeasies with gangsters and jazz musicians on Friday nights. So domestic work was not something she
understood or cared about. From what I can recall, she would go
from messy room to messy room, standing in the doorways with
her hands on her hips, sighing in confusion.

George would wake up every morning, shower and shave, and
then he and Bunny would sit around the kitchen drinking coffee
and eating toast. The radio would be playing as well—CFRB,

news, weather, sports, mouthy commentators like Gordon Sinclair and Pierre Berton. I would hear them from my room down the hall. I'd lie in bed until George was ready to go. He would say goodbye and head down the stairs to a taxi idling in the driveway waiting for him. I would wave to him from the front as he went around the corner. Even though he was blind he would wave back before disappearing down Brucedale Avenue. Bunny would throw a couple of Pop-Tarts in the toaster and pour me a glass of orange juice and maybe a cup of tea before I got dressed myself and headed out the door and north up 36th Street to Peace Memorial School.

Peace Memorial sat between Queensdale Avenue and Crockett Street on East 36th. The school was built after World War I and then expanded to accommodate the baby boom after World War II, with two huge wings spreading the building north to south over a city block. The driveway to the teachers' parking lot bordered on Munn Street, the heart of a post-war housing development. Tiny wood-framed two-bedroom cottages, families with six kids living in and pouring out of them all day and all night long.

Munn Street was where the tough kids lived. Walter Stadnick, a famous Hells Angel, came off that street. He may have been the most notorious figure from our neighbourhood. Guys like Walter were born to be wild on Munn Street. Gangs of kids hung out at the Peace Memorial schoolyard—smoking cigarettes, feeling up their girlfriends, sniffing glue and forming a rodeo of stolen bikes. About three houses south off Munn Street on the corner of East 36th and Queensdale was the site of the hand-to-hand battles that happened every morning at eight and every afternoon at four. The crowds would follow two opponents up the streets shouting a long chorus of fiiiiiiiight!!!! The parade would end on the side lawn of the Kingdom Hall, and the swinging and kicking and blood and tears would start.

These fights usually involved kids from "the opportunity class," who ran a little slow and who had no chance in a regular classroom. They were the victims of and the entertainment for the rest of the school. They were like the Christians in the Roman Colosseum. They served to keep the mob happy.

I had my own gang of inseparable misfits. My house was the last one on our route to school. Every morning, Ken Peters, Mark Stringer and Doug Crawford would bang on my front door. Bunny was always wary of visitors, but she welcomed these three. They were my best friends. We talked about girls and sports. Together we were all shocked when Kenny Churm told us about the facts of life, explaining that babies were made by our moms and dads rubbing their dinks together. We all paused and stared out over the rooftops on East 36th Street. Impossible. No way that happens. We were interested in the world from a distance, like it was unattainable and not for guys like us from the East Mountain.

I realized I was "poor" around the age of six or seven. Before that age I had no idea. The world has to tell you. The same way the world tells you that you're fat or your nose is too big. You really don't know these things until some dick points it out to you. I remember Jackie Washington telling me about the first time he realized he was black, or at least that he was someone different who was assigned a name to go along with his colour. He was playing with a bunch of kids after school in the North End, and they were all running away from one another, pointing and shouting "nigger, nigger." Jackie joined in but soon realized that they were running away from him. That they were pointing at him and shouting "nigger" at him. He was devastated. He broke away from the group and cried all the way home.

Two incidents illustrated where I stood in the world, and both of those incidents occurred at Christmastime.

The first was the Christmas Eve when Bunny, not having the funds to buy toys, panicked and wrapped up household items to put under our tree instead. The next morning, I unwrapped the old hammer Bunny kept in the kitchen drawer with her knives and forks. The hammer was her father's. It had a wooden handle and a well-worn head that was a bit wobbly. Bunny claimed her father, Orlando, could fix anything. She told me she used to climb up on the roof with him, handing him nails, holding down shingles and getting his lunch. She'd assist him reframing doors and preparing the storm windows for cold Quebec winters. I was aware even at a young age of what this hammer meant to Bunny. I knew she had given it to me in an act of desperation. I also knew the hammer would be back in the kitchen drawer by afternoon.

I reached under the tree and continued to unwrap the rest of the presents labelled to me: Johnson's baby powder, a bottle of George's Aqua Velva, a 1940s Bostitch office stapler and two pairs of socks I'd never seen before. I understood the effort that had been made. I could feel Bunny's pain at not having the money to buy Christmas presents, though Janie did show up from Toronto later that day with a Hot Wheels track and cars.

The second incident took place in December of 1966, when I was in grade one and Peace Memorial was visited by the Salvation Army, who, during an assembly in the school gym, preached the importance of putting together "Christmas hampers" for "the needy." The next day after the morning bell, the office announcements, the Lord's Prayer and "God Save the Queen," our teacher Mrs. Meyer stood at the front of the class and announced that Christmas was just around the corner and that some Hamiltonians were not as fortunate as our families were. Some boys and girls had fathers who didn't have jobs, and their families did not have any money for toys and Christmas trees and decorations. These boys and girls, she told us, often went to bed hungry. These families would not even have a Christmas dinner. She too referred to these families as "the needy," a term that seemed to ignite the young minds of my grade-one class as well as the rest of the school, all the way up to the grade sixes. That recess, the playground was all in a flutter about The Needy.

Where did they live?

Where were they from?

What did they look like?

To be fair, we didn't have much to go on. Stan Nixon, whose father was a mechanic and whose entire family lived in a small trailer on a lot two streets over on East 39th Street, said The Needy were "niggers" and "Indians." I knew what Indians were because my uncle John was an Indian and so was my aunt's boyfriend, Jim Beauvais, but I had never heard the word *nigger* before. I thought I might try it out on Bunny. We were crossing Upper Gage with George and our dog, and I hurled the word at the cars speeding past us. I was met with a swat to the back of the head. "Don't let me ever hear you saying that horrible word again, do you understand me."

But back in the playground, during fifteen-minute-long recess, The Needy were demonized to the level of thieves, Nazis, and monsters. A simple game of tag was transformed from "you're It" to "you're Needy." The playground would go wild, with kids running for their lives from the one needy loser who scrambled over the cracked post-war concrete, tackling the slowest of the pack, dragging them down like a scene from *Ben-Hur*. Ripped flesh, scuffed shoes and tears were followed by taunts of "You're the Needy, You're the Needy."

So even though a certain amount of thoughtfulness was extended to The Needy in the classroom, in the playground they took a beating twice a day at recess.

December rolled along. Christmas decorations were constructed and hung, carols were sung, and in the corner of our classroom, by the front door and beside the chalkboard, was an old Dominion cardboard box decorated with wrapping paper, and in that box we would put our food for The Needy. Mrs. Meyer had announced to the class that some of The Needy didn't have stoves, fridges or pots and pans, and so it was good to bring in instant (just-add-water) kinds of food. Rice, potatoes, instant milk, pudding and cans of fruit and vegetables were best. Kraft Dinner, spaghetti and cereal were perfect needy-people items.

No stove?

No fridge?

"What the fuck?" laughed Stan Nixon. "Who don't got a stove? Who the fuck don't got a fridge?"

Fuck. Fuck? Another word to try out on Bunny, I thought, having not learned my lesson.

When the Christmas holidays arrived, our classroom's hamper was overflowing with cans and boxes and cartons of army-issue-style food rations. I of course did my part to help. Bunny gave me a paper bag of canned corn, Kraft Dinner and instant milk to add to the box. I felt good about helping out. I felt good about what I had because Bunny always made sure I was thankful for what I received.

I ran out the back door of Peace Memorial on December 20 feeling a mix of relief and freedom and excitement that Santa was coming and that I would not have to be bothered with adding and subtracting and reading and The Needy and Stan Nixon's words that got me in trouble every time.

A day or two later there was a knock at the door. Trixie jumped off the couch and ferociously attacked the inside door knob, and Bunny dried her hands on her apron, walked across the kitchen and opened the door. There were two men in uniform standing there with the snow falling all around them. Bunny yelled at me, "Hold the dog. . . . Hold Trixie back, for Christ's sake." One of the men handed Bunny a box and graciously wished her and her family a merry Christmas. Bunny put the box on the kitchen table, and I ran in behind her excited to see what magical gift the two men in uniform had brought. She told me to get back, but I kneeled on a chair beside her, leaning over the kitchen table waiting to see what was inside. Bunny pulled back the cardboard flaps and revealed a card that said, "Seasons Greetings from your Salvation Army." Deeper inside the box were cans and boxes of food.

I was confused. What kind of gift was this?

I reached in and pulled out a can of Green Giant Niblets Corn. Wow, I thought. That's the same kind of canned corn I brought in for the Christmas hamper at school. I stared at it some more. Then I stared past it into the rest of the box and saw instant milk, cans of spaghetti sauce and beans.

What was going on here?

Why was this box of food brought to our door?

Until that night I'd had no idea what poor people looked like. I sat in the silence around our kitchen table and looked at

Bunny and George and stared down at my plate. I knew who I was then. I was one of The Needy.

THE WAR AMPS POOL

Most of the social events Bunny and George dragged me to were held at assorted Legions, veterans clubs and the Canadian National Institute for the Blind. The War Amps on the mountain brow was the closest club to our rented house on East 36th Street. It's where I would be taken to swim from time to time in the summer as a young boy, and at Christmas it's where I'd go to get my presents from Santa.

Children of broken World War II veterans would gather for Remembrance Days, Easters, Christmas parties. These gatherings were a chance for the vets to drink and bitch and watch the Leafs and Ticat games together, and for the aging war brides to drink and complain and talk about what was happening on *Coronation Street*. As a young fella, I saw it as the best of times for all of them.

The War Amps club was an old house on the edge of the Hamilton escarpment at the end of East 34th Street, on land granted by the Queen to the boys who gave so much in the fight against "those nasty Germans." It was a Garden of Eden for working-class war heroes, I suppose, a break in the action, a place to lay down the swords and join the family. The house was on a treed lawn bordered by a short stone wall. There was a parking lot, some picnic tables and a swimming pool.

Oh god . . . the swimming pool.

My first trip to the swimming pool was when I was six years old. Our family didn't own a car, so Bunny and I walked down East 36th Street and over to the brow in the blistering afternoon heat. It was the sixties and everything I wore in the summer was polyester and came in Hot Wheels colours. Lime-green bathing suit, spectra-flame tank top, antifreeze sun hat. I looked like I had rolled right off the Mattel assembly line, a walking version of Big Daddy Roth's Beatnik Bandit.

I remember Bunny giving me a little history lesson about the pool as we walked up the steps towards the smell of chlorine and cigarette smoke. "This is the pool that Harry Cockman's crippled son committed suicide in by tying himself to his wheel-chair and rolling his wheels towards the edge of the concrete bunker filled with water. He drowned and sank to the bottom until the grounds maintenance man found him the next morning. Poor wee fella."

It's also where blind veteran Dino Rocco stripped down and stumbled onto the diving board, then, running full speed off the board and into a dive, landed on the concrete at the bottom of the—yes—empty pool. Rocco broke his neck and died there. After surviving two years in a Japanese POW camp, tortured by his captors and nearly starved to death, Rocco met his end right there on the floor of the empty war-vets swimming pool. Needless to say, I was terrified as we approached my maiden swim at the pool. Bunny's timing was always spot-on when it came to telling horror stories.

The most unthinkable stories she would save for supper time. She couldn't help herself. Tales of train wrecks, body parts, mob hits, Hiroshima, Kennedy's day in Dallas, priests and altar boys, white slavery, shotgun suicides—all got thrown out across my plate of meatloaf and boiled potatoes, the bloody condiment to otherwise boring meals.

I stood there in my lime-green bathing suit for a long, long time with the August sun beating down on me before I finally found the courage to jump in. As the cool water took hold of me, I could imagine poor Cockman's wheelchair below me. I screamed underwater but no one heard me. I swam to the surface and saw Bunny poolside in a camp chair reading the *Hamilton Spectator* and smoking a Rothmans. I screamed again. She looked across the water at me for a moment and went back to the news.

Inside, the club was dark and dreary and filled with smoke and the smell of piss and beer and dried blood. Blind men and men missing arms or legs would gather to drink and often fight in the dimly lit room. Shuffleboard tables and pictures of Queen Elizabeth, Lester B. Pearson and King George hung on faded wallpaper. Nobody ever stopped to look at those pictures. Ever.

I was the youngest of the WWII kids, due to Bunny and George having become parents late in their lives. I was flung into a group of vets' grandchildren, some orphans and assorted child amputees from around the region.

We'd be brought to the War Amps club to ring in the Christmas season in style. Santa was a guy named Jack Fairfax. He dressed in the well-worn Santa suit, strung the beard around his gin-blossomed cheeks and stuck a black glove on the stump of his left arm. He manoeuvred the gifts from a big bag with his one good arm and his only hand, while his assistant, Mrs. Fairfax, bellowed the names of the lucky children across the bar. Santa smoked Player's and drank Molson Export stubbies.

What a mess. But the vets' hearts were in the right place. They had come marching home from war a fraction of the men they were before they left. They continued to fight addictions and poverty and shitty jobs, and still every year they would pull together their version of a Christmas party for some kids with less than normal lives. Way to go, boys.

There was no money for a babysitter, so I accompanied Bunny and George to War Amps dinners at hotel ballrooms in Hamilton and Toronto. I would be dressed in bow tie and blazer and forced to sit through speeches and awards and beer and rye, and sometimes a band would play some old country classics or Vera Lynn tearjerker. "White Cliffs of Dover," "When the Moon Comes Over the Mountain," "Tennessee Waltz," "Red River Valley," etc., etc.

When I got a little older, around nine or ten years old, I was usually sat at a table with the annual "Timmy." Timmy was a young person who, due to an unfortunate accident, had lost a limb, just like the big boys from WWII. He was put up on posters and dragged out to War Amps events and shopping centres and presented at schools as an example of what can happen if you fuck around and act like a careless daredevil.

The speakers and dignitaries at these dinners would sit at the head table at the front of the room. In front of that head table, exposed to the entire room, was a smaller one with just two chairs. As a spotlight shone down on him, Timmy would be paraded in and led to the little table.

"There he is folks—Timmy." The wives applauded and the old men dragged their forks across their plates searching for a carrot or a pea, or sat back and poured whisky over their gums and banged their canes on the hardwood floor while Timmy limped by.

I would be brought over to Timmy's table and introduced to him. The crowd would ooh and aah, and I would take my seat across from Timmy. We'd sit there in complete silence eating our roast beef and carrots and extra kid-helpings of dessert. We would both act like it was not happening. Like nothing was happening. Like the world had stopped and we were invisible.

Here are a few facts about the annual Timmy:
Fact:

- Timmy was an understandably miserable kid who had lost an arm or a leg doing some foolish shit like playing with blasting caps at a construction site or trying to hop on a moving train.
- Timmy was, nine times out of ten, a peewee hockey star before his accident, although I had no way of proving this annoying fact. And because I was such a lousy skater myself, I never acted impressed by this potential NHLer's poor luck. In fact, I was a bit pissed off that this kid threw away a chance to stickhandle and shoot a puck with amazing ease just so he could impress some girls or some buddies or, even worse, pick up on a dare from his so-called friends.
- Every time, the train will take the leg.
- Every time, the blasting caps will take the arm.
- Every time, I prayed to God that no more kids would lose any more limbs, just so I didn't have to sit and eat another meal in silence under a white spotlight in a ballroom full of tired old men and women eating roast beef.

I prayed that no more kids would have to be named Timmy and used as an example to show the world how unforgiving life can be to those whose luck runs out early. I prayed I would grow up fast and forget all this, but I guess my luck ran out.

TAILGUNNER WILSON

George Wilson was a farm boy, a lacrosse player, a wanderer, a banker, a prospector, an RCAF flight sergeant, a tail gunner, a blind man, a father and a mystery.

George fought the Germans from the suicide seat of a Lancaster bomber. It was the seat of no return. He had to have been a madman to take that job. Or maybe he had a death wish that he kept between himself and the blackness that surrounded him every night high above Europe. Whatever it was that made him sit down in the rear end of that giant RCAF Lancaster, he made sure none of us would ever know about it. It would stay locked up in George's head with the morphine, the steel plate that covered the hole above his right temple, the English tarts he'd frequent in London and all his other wishes and secrets. (Bunny found a photo that George had

carried home with him after the war. She'd pull it out and show it
to me and tell me it was "your father's girlfriend.")

George Wilson was a war hero. And like most war heroes,
he arrived home a broken man. In those days, there was no feel-
good therapy or self-help books. He found himself a stool at
the bar of the newly opened El Mocambo on Spadina Avenue in
Toronto and dove into the bottle. He loved booze before the
war, but lived for it when he came home, dumped on the streets
of Toronto blind and crazy with a major head injury. He'd drink
at the kitchen table, he'd drink in Legions and he'd drink in
hotel rooms at War Amps conventions.

He'd knock 'em back with his blind war vet buddies and
sometimes with a larger collection of warriors who were missing
arms and legs, as well as one guy named Smitty, who was missing
his nose. And after George had one too many, the surgical scars
left by the hospital in France would cut loose and the left side of
his face would lose its nerve, leaving George's mouth to droop
and his speech to slur. George looked and sounded like he had a
stroke in these moments, and Bunny was always the first to notice.

She was quick to fly off her chair on the other side of the
room and rush around looking for something for George to
chew. A crust of bread would work, or other times it would be
a piece of wood or a facecloth, a toothpick or a match cover.
The movement of chewing would reactivate the muscles and
bring him back to some kind of acceptable appearance while
continuing on with his drunkenness.

George's temper used to shock people because when he
was sober he was soft spoken and timid as a church mouse.
After the whisky and the beer hit the metal plate in his head, all
hell would break loose. Blind George took on all comers. Bar
stools would fly and jaws get cracked. He managed to do a fair

amount of damage up and down Spadina Avenue, much to the surprise of bartenders, bouncers and onlookers who pretty well let him do whatever he wanted because he was a war hero and had lost so much fighting those soulless Germans. He won back our freedom, so he got free rein over every room he entered, which was a pretty good deal for him.

But Bunny suffered many long nights. There was no calming him down once he got home. He was a tiger in a cage. A tiger in a cage with a plate in its head and a cane to swing around. The walls of their little apartment on Huron Street had holes in the plaster from George trying to beat some light into his pitch-black world. His anguished cries were heard over the treetops and across the football field of Varsity Stadium and finally lost their power and crash-landed like George's Lancaster bomber on the lawn of Queen's Park.

Bunny and George moved to Hamilton in the fifties so George could settle into his job at a confectionery stand in a downtown post office. By the time I ended up running around his rented house on East 36th Street in Hamilton, he was a little older, a little tired and not so prone to the raging anger and violent outbursts that went along with having your eyesight robbed from you at the age of thirty.

The red-brick bungalow Bunny and George rented faced east, second from the northwest corner of Brucedale and East 36th Street. Our house, 162 East 36th Street, was the wreck of the block, all overgrown lawn and broken windows, and there was nobody in the house capable of fixing even the smallest problem, so whatever was broken would stay that way for eternity.

In those days, Hamilton's East Mountain was in various stages of development. There were old farmhouses with the old people living in them still holding their own. There were wood-framed wartime houses, four-room cottages, usually with five or six kids stuffed in them, and then there were the piles of dirt and wood and bricks and beer bottles, where families in trailers lived, waiting for their houses to be built.

There were also some houses with perfect little lawns and gardens and fresh paint and washed cars and aprons and Trillium Awards displayed by the front doors. The folks in these houses needed to define themselves. They clung to middle-class attitudes to separate themselves from the armies of working-class, welfare and biker families that had settled in the neighbourhood from downtown and out of town and far away to come and work in the steel factories.

George did not have too much to say about the war or his enemy, the Germans. Bunny, on the other hand, had lots of anger and plenty to say about a nation of people who had set up camps to kill children and their innocent families, dropped bombs on England and taken her husband's eyes away. Her book collection grew, with paperbacks of *Treblinka*, *Rise and Fall of the Third Reich* and *The Holocaust Kingdom*. She would go into detail at dinnertime with excerpts of unthinkable, mindless violence and unexplainable evil that always ended with "those bloody Germans."

I went to bed in fear and woke up in fear that the Germans would break through time and space and pull up in front of 162 East 36th Street with their tanks and lederhosen and flame throwers and try to take my eyes away from me. I had a list of the scariest monsters known to my preschool mind. In ascending order:

6. Lee Harvey Oswald
5. Alfred Hitchcock
4. Sharks

3. Perry Edward Smith and Richard Hickock, the two
guys who kill the Clutter family in Truman Capote's
In Cold Blood—At the age of four, I accidentally
watched that movie when Bunny and George had
fallen asleep.

2. Frankenstein's monster

1. The Germans

One morning Bunny saw a moving van pull onto our street
and a new family move into the Masons' old house, six doors
up. She inquired among the other housewives about who the
new neighbours were and where they were from. That night at
dinner the answer came back like an anti-aircraft missile tearing
through our kitchen.

Germans...

Germans had moved onto our street. I expected my father
to go to the basement and unpack machine guns and bayonets,
and my mother, in her apron, to lay out a map of Hamilton's
East Mountain on the kitchen table for us to plan our attack.
I thought tunnels would be dug and barbed wire strung around
the perimeter of our house to ensure no Germans could sneak
up and spy on us through our bedroom windows.

But none of this happened. Instead I lay awake in my
mother's bed every night, wide-eyed and terrified until CFRB's
Starlight Serenade faded over and out and I was carried away
by the transistor radio in the kitchen, cradled to sleep and
away from the Germans by host George Wilson (not my
George Wilson) and Rimsky-Korsakov, Chopin, Puccini, Vaughan
Williams and Sibelius.

Still, from a safe distance the Germans were watched day in,
day out as they unpacked their cardboard boxes, teak furniture,

appliances and winter tires. "The whole neighbourhood is talk-ing," said Bunny at the dinner table. It comforted me that we were not alone, that the Keiths, Montes, Tessaros, Baldassarios and all brave Canadians would be on guard for me.

Questions were raised about the Germans of East 36th Street. Had their family or their fellow villagers back home in the fatherland turned local Jews in to the Nazi authorities? Had they discovered any downed Allied paratroopers hiding in their barns? Had they killed them with pitchforks when they did? The parents were met with polite smiles, of course, but the young boy, Alfred, endured the brunt of our kitchen table suspicions. He was teased for the way he spoke, forbidden from playing street hockey with us, beaten up and, finally, stripped and tied to a telephone pole one night during a game of hide and seek.

The war was over but the battle raged on. The kids on East 36th Street had all seen the good guy vs bad guy, Germans vs Us movies like *The Great Escape* and *Stalag 17* and every Tuesday tuned into *Combat!*, the weekly Hollywood account of World War II starring Vic Morrow. I ended up befriending Alfred, and even though I could not sway the mob's opinion, I can at least say I gave him a chance to breathe a bit easier know-ing he had one friend on the block.

Andy Strang was our neighbour. His alcohol-induced Jekyll and Hyde routine kept his family in constant fear. He threw his wife's cooking out their kitchen window onto Brucedale Avenue and he pissed in her cedar chest at the end of their bed on a regular basis. Once, he put his son Archie's head though the liv-ing room wall, an incident that became a domestic violence legend on our street, or at least next door in our house.

"Go to bed now or I'll put your head through the wall like Mr. Strang did to Archie's," Bunny would say. "Do your homework or I'll put your head through the wall like Mr. Strang did to Archie's." "Clean up your toys or . . ." It was the sixties after all, and other people's misfortune could be used to enforce fear and inspire a work ethic. A threat for all occasions, you might say.

In addition to several drunken moments throughout the year, Mr. Strang made an annual visit to our house on Christmas Eve, when he would enter the house, bounce off the walls and into a chair at the kitchen table, where George Wilson would pour him rum until his head hit the table and he pissed on the kitchen floor.

"Bunny . . . I pissed on your floor," Strang would announce. Bunny would grab a mop and some soapy water, and Strang would bounce off a few more walls, out the front door and out into the night.

Bunny loved everything about mob life. Maybe because when she was a child the famous Legs Diamond hid out in her hometown, taking the local kids for rides in his Cadillac and buying them soda pops. She loved to gossip about mobsters, mob hits, mob hangouts. Hamilton provided her lots to fuel her obsession. Everybody knew somebody who knew somebody who grew up with, worked for or got worked over by Johnny Pops. Johnny Papalia that is, sometime local kingpin, monster and much-feared enforcer of the Southern Ontario mafia. His power reached up to Montreal and down through Buffalo to New York City, making Hamilton a hotbed of fun, drugs, frontier justice and foulmouthed streetwise banter that otherwise could only be heard coming from Hollywood gangsters on the big screen. Bunny had a front-row seat to it all and she loved every minute of it.

Bunny tended to group all Italians into the mobster category and as a result kept a close eye on some of our Italian neighbours. Out of this came an index finger wet with dishwater that pointed directly across the street to Jimmy Monte. Bunny estimated that Jimmy was a low-ranking diabetic mobster in the Johnny Papalia crew. He was notorious for not taking his insulin and falling into a coma, usually to be found by his son Bobby when he arrived home for lunch from Blessed Sacrament school. Jimmy and his family were the first ticket scalpers in the city. The first ones I knew of, anyway. He always had tickets to sports events, plays, concerts, in venues from Toronto to Buffalo. His wife, Andrea, had a table at the Royal York's Imperial Room in Toronto for any show she wanted to see—Al Martino, Anne Murray, Bobby Vinton.

Andrea was kinda boy crazy. She worked as a cashier at the Dominion store at Gage and Fennell along with a handful of other boy-crazy neighbourhood women. They all had crushes on the shelf stockers, delivery truck drivers and customers who buzzed around the grocery store. If Jimmy had got wind of Andrea's crushes, he could have had any and all of these unsuspecting men disappear into the Hamilton harbour to swim with Rocco Perri.

Jimmy's kids loved him and so did I, even though looking back he was really just a grumpy Italian guy. Jimmy would sometimes glance across East 36th Street, see me hanging around on my front porch and take me along with his kids, Teresa and Bobby, and their cousins to things like the Hell Drivers at the CNE and the Shrine Circus and the Ice Capades, and one time we all went to the Hamilton Forum to see Little Joe (Michael Landon), star of *Bonanza*, in person along with a real rodeo. Bunny dressed me like I was going to my first communion, in a black blazer, red vest and a tie, and warned me to stay close to the Monte clan because there were going to be a lot of "homos" down there at the Forum waiting to steal young boys and take them into bathroom stalls and "bugger" them. (Mind you, the way Bunny had me dressed I looked like the belle of the ball for every pedophile north of Barton Street.)

I took this advice to heart, and even though I didn't know what she was talking about I thought the words "bugger" and "homo" did not sound too good. They were mystery words like the words Stan Nixon spit out in the schoolyard.

One time I went with Jimmy and his relatives to a Ticat game at old Civic Stadium, and after the game he took us all down to the locker room to meet Angelo Mosca. I remember Jimmy guiding us past the weak security and down into the bowels of the stadium. The hallways were concrete blocks and the lighting was dim. It was like a scene out of an old black-and-white movie: we were like gangsters on our way to pay off a boxer under the ring before the fight. In reality, though, we were a gangster with neighbourhood kids going down to meet the CFL defensive lineman.

We walked into the Tiger Cats' dressing room, and Mosca was right there before us in a towel eating a plate of chicken and pasta out of a Tupperware container that his wife must have packed for him. He was not so friendly to us kids, but he was all smiles for Jimmy. They disappeared to talk about something or other in Italian, and we just stood there in the middle of a room of naked football idols. Tommy Joe Coffey, Joe Zuger, Garney Henley . . . it was like my CFL football card collection coming to life. Naked.

Jimmy never went to a job like the other dads. He just went out late at night. Bunny would keep tabs on him through our kitchen window. "Ah . . . there he goes . . . runnin' around town for Johnny," she'd say while she did the dishes. Later, she would stand in the dark kitchen in her underwear and apron waiting for him to return. I'd get up to go pee in the middle of the night and hear CHML softly playing Glen Campbell or CFRB's *Starlight Serenade*. "Shhh," she'd say. "Jimmy is out working for the mob tonight. I am waiting to see what he unloads from his car." I imagined him digging holes up on Limeridge Road under cover of darkness and dumping loan-sharked deadbeats and rival gang members from the trunk of that Pontiac. But mostly I think he drove his green Parisienne around in the middle of the night picking up party girls and sandwiches for the big boys at their card games down at the Connaught Hotel.

A VOICE THAT RARELY GETS HEARD

I used to sneak into Bunny and George's bedroom, where secret treasures of their past lay on the floor, in the closet and hidden in the pages of the Wilson family Bible. I discovered that in the top drawer of her dresser Bunny kept an old wallet that had belonged to her brother-in-law John Lazare, a chief on the Kahnawake Mohawk Reserve who was once married to Bunny's sister Isabelle. Inside the wallet was a black-and-white photo of my cousin Janie as a little girl, maybe four or five years old, holding a fluffy dog. Janie loved animals. I think she saw herself in them. She protected dogs on the rez from stone-throwing little fuckers who treated these animals like they didn't deserve to live, like they didn't have hearts pleading through their eyes. Janie saw their hearts. Janie stepped up for little creatures that couldn't defend themselves. I would sit and stare at the photo. I could see Janie. Really see her, staring back into the camera and out of the photo at me. I was drawn to the innocence and the beauty I saw in the picture. In it Janie looked free.

Janie was nineteen years older than me, but even when I was a child, I knew her life had not been easy. The black-and-white photo was taken before school kids on the reserve recognized her as half them and half the others. The others. The French. Everywhere she stepped, Janie carried generations of the enemy on her back. The photo was taken before Janie's mother made her feel guilty for growing breasts too early. Before her mother, without giving a reason, alienated Janie from her father and her sister, Millie. Isabelle was a brutal, controlling woman. The little girl didn't stand a chance.

I also knew that I was not the first child Bunny had cared for. Janie was. Bunny's loyalty and love for Janie were deep. Bunny was there when Janie was born. She reached into her sister Isabelle and delivered a baby who was underweight and sick, and Janie stayed that way through her childhood. She was taken for x-ray after x-ray after x-ray when she was a child in Quebec, but her doctor there was unable to help her in any lasting way. On one occasion when Bunny came to visit, she intervened. "I'm taking Janie," Bunny told John Lazare. "This little girl is going to be dead within the year if she stays here any longer." So Bunny packed Janie up and took her to Sick Kids in Toronto. She was in Toronto for six and a half years. They needed to build up her strength and weight, and when she was strong enough she had a lung removed. Bunny cared for her the whole time.

Two of Bunny's sisters—Isabelle and Pearl—married Mohawk men, but Bunny coached Janie to deny that side of her heritage. If Bunny, George and Janie were out together, at a War Amps dinner, down at the Legion or at George's confectionery, and someone asked Janie where she was visiting from, Bunny would barge in between them, interrupt and answer so that everyone around could hear, "This is our niece, Jane Lazare. She's visiting from Montreal. She is my sister's daughter." So even Bunny's kindness towards Janie came with an edge.

When she was fifteen, Janie got a job at Sammy's, the grocery store on the reserve. On Fridays Janie would finish her shift and roll a shopping cart up and down the aisles to top up her family's kitchen cupboards. One Friday, she returned home with her arms full of groceries. She came in through the kitchen door to find the family sitting, eating dinner at the table. Following Isabelle's instructions, nobody spoke to Janie and nobody looked at her. Not even her father, which surprised and hurt Janie the most. Janie sat in the rocking chair by the front window of the house with her bags of groceries at her feet and thought, "Okay, if this is how it's going to go, then, I bought food and I'll make my own dinner." She reached in the bag, opened up a package of Montreal smoked meat and a loaf of bread, went back into the kitchen and boiled some water, made some instant coffee, went back to the rocking chair, sat down and ate her dinner. Janie stayed there in silence every morning before work and every night after, as her family talked and ate and laughed and went about their business, for three months. She was never told why she was treated this way for so long.

Bunny had four sisters: Madeline, Doris, Pearl and Isabelle. Isabelle was a particularly dark and venomous woman, but they were all a competitive and cutthroat brood, quick tongued and silver threaded, ready to brawl at the drop of a hat. And they came by their disposition honestly: Irish and French and hidden Mohawk blood running through their veins, and every one of them stunningly beautiful. Their Irish mother, Beatrice, lined them up and struck them across their backsides with a wooden stick to ready them for a cold, cold world. A world Beatrice knew well.

Bunny loved to tell me the story of how her mother, Beatrice Neeland, met her father, Orlando St. James. She would break into a smile before launching gleefully into the romantic tale of her parents' magical union. Though it has to be said the story was a little sparse and sketchy:

One night, when Bunny's mother was just a teenager, she was with two men in a car parked on a dark country road near Ville La Salle, when one of the men got fresh with her. He attacked her, but she was tough and feisty and she beat him off, swung the car door open and jumped to freedom, tearing down the road to the first farmhouse in view, her attacker in close pursuit. Out of breath from leaping over snowbanks, she frantically banged at the door, her small frozen hands almost shattering on impact, her dress torn and her makeup smeared across her face. Bunny's dad, Orlando, answered the door in his one-piece long underwear. He was six feet three inches tall and had the build of a working man. A train man, to be exact. He'd been shovelling coal and swinging hammers all his life. He looked like a giant raging ghost with a face full of shaving cream and talcum powder, waving a straight razor over his head and screaming and spitting in French as he chased the men off, down the icy mud road.

I never had any reason to question Bunny's story when I was a kid. It was exciting and romantic like it was pulled from a Nancy Drew novel. She told it with pauses built in for giggles and laughter. The same pauses every time.

Of course, what went unsaid in this story of love at first

sight was what Bunny's mother was doing on that dark road in that car with two men to begin with. What was never mentioned in this fairytale was that mother Neeland was a resourceful crook who apparently had her daughters out earning on the streets of Montreal at an early age. Beatrice Neeland just may have been turning tricks and robbing johns for some time. She learned these skills from her brutal Irish mother. The same mother who ordered some of her sons into the Montreal police force, knowing that having a silver badge, a legal gun and a "shoot first, ask questions later" policy on her side would buffer the family's dark dealings. Others escaped their mother's reach, joined the army and died fighting overseas in World War I. Their pictures hung in every Neeland home, and they were carried by Bunny's grandmother to mass every Sunday.

After Beatrice and Orlando were married, the Neelands went on to terrorize the St. James family. Over the years, they robbed Orlando's house and his dairy business, raided his garden, stole cars and drank any bottle of booze they could get their hands on. Bunny and her sisters were forbidden from visiting the Neelands at their home in Montreal for fear they might be sold off into white slavery down in Chinatown. Perhaps it's not surprising then that Isabelle ended up somewhat cruel and warped.

When she could, Janie left Kahnawake, and as I was growing up she was always around. She'd come in from Toronto to attend events of any significance: communions and hockey playoffs, and later she and Bunny would come to my concerts and shows at festivals and in theatres. Janie was a bit like Ed McMahon on *The Tonight Show Starring Johnny Carson*. Nobody really knew what Ed was doing there on TV every night, but Johnny always had him to bounce his zingers off. Janie was Bunny's sidekick.

She always stood a few feet behind Bunny. Bunny would say her piece and then Janie might respond with a laugh or a head shake or sometimes a few words, words that were often lost in the crowd of conversation buzzing around us. Janie's was a voice that was rarely heard. There's plenty of heartbreak in a voice that rarely gets heard.

DEATH RATTLE SUNSET

In the summertime, Bunny and George used to shut the house down after supper. Bunny didn't trust me in my own bed, so she'd make me get into bed with her on the pullout sofa in the front room. How depressing it was to lie wide awake in bed with the sun still full in the sky, listening to the "normals," the neighbourhood families in their yards, with their puffy, red-faced boozy friends dropping over, barbecuing and snapping the tops off bottles of beer with church keys, and kids laughing and fighting, and wives getting drunk and smoking cigarettes around the cheap metal patio furniture and picnic tables, gossiping about the heathen Protestants and whether there'd be a strike at Stelco next year and about who was stepping out on who around the block and up the street at O'Hannigans' drugstore, about the dirty details of the cashiers and the managers in the stockrooms at the Dominion store. Meanwhile, in my house the very last sounds of the day came from down the hall, where George Wilson lay alone in his own bed in his own darkness away from Bunny and me. George kept a transistor radio beside his bed. He would lean in towards the tiny speaker and tune in the news. The voice of Ray Sonin. The dim light of the radio dial. My first signs of how lonely life can be. What was it about the monotone male newsreader that made me feel like I didn't belong, like there was so much going on that had nothing to do with me?

When I was four years old I stood in Bunny's kitchen, three feet tall, and came right out with what was on my mind: Why did I not look anything like Bunny and George? And why were they so old? Bunny was quick to tell me I should be happy with who and where I was. I stopped asking for a while after that.

There were, however, bold, mouthy, confident kids in the Peace Memorial schoolyard and up and down East 36th Street who were happy to tell me to my face that I looked different. They talked to me like there were no mirrors in my house to see it for myself. We had mirrors, but somehow I could stand in front of the one in the bathroom, brushing my teeth and combing my hair before school, and no longer see what they saw. They'd ask me if Bunny and George were my real parents or if they were my grandparents. They asked me if I was adopted. They asked me the questions I didn't dare ask myself, questions that more often than not ended in fist fights.

I was on my own out there. I tried to divert their attention away from me. I made up stories that Bunny and George were secret agents, working undercover looking for the Germans. I focused on George's blindness and his war-hero status. I became the kid with the blind father instead of the kid with the giant head, and that suited me fine. I lost myself in a dreamland to avoid being seen.

I doubted myself. I didn't have any confidence. I compensated by acting up. My report cards often read, "Tommy plays the clown to get attention from his fellow students." I sang in class, out loud, all the time I'm told. My daydreams became one-act plays with me running around the classroom, through jungles like I was Tarzan or Sergeant Rock or the Hulk. I couldn't control myself.

Teachers would drag Bunny into the school to report on my odd behaviour. They told her that I should be put back a grade or two or put in the slow class, which led to the opportunity class, which led to Crestwood Vocational School, then maybe even Mounthaven, where the slow kids went. I was on a downward spiral and I was just seven years old. Hell, I was just getting started.

Teachers would move my desk around the classroom to keep an eye on me. I'd start out in the general population, then get moved to the back of the class where I would be isolated. But that didn't work, so I'd be told to move my desk right beside the teacher's desk so that I'd never be out of her sight or reach. Eventually I'd end up with my desk out in the hallway. I'd have to listen in on the classroom through the doorway. The voices in the morning saying the Lord's Prayer and singing "God Save the Queen" melted into the sound of chalk against the blackboard and then just the sound of pencil lead on notebook paper. My assignments were usually delivered to my desk by cute girls like Patti Wilk or Lynn Harris. I loved it, the voices and footsteps that echoed off the walls up the long hallway. I'd nap and dream and doodle the days away. If this was punishment I was all in.

I soon figured out that I could wander away from my post outside the classroom and get lost in the massive old school. I'd dodge any teachers in the halls, hit the stairs and descend into the basement under the original structure to the boiler room and the old coal chutes that led down to the furnace-room killing floor. I followed the tunnels under the new wings, into the film room and the bomb shelters that were built after the war. It was a fantasy land and a walk through history at the same time.

I'd run into Ted Wren, the janitor at the school. He'd give me a wink and let me know that I was out of bounds but that he wasn't going to tell anyone. I knew Ted Wren as a professional wrestler. A local fall guy, no less. He would get his ass kicked during bouts of not-so-well-rehearsed choreography that always ended with Wren bleeding and pinned to the mat in the centre of the Hamilton Forum by all the ridiculous wrestling greats of that era. Haystacks Calhoun, the Love Brothers, the Sheik—not the Iron Sheik, the original Sheik, with his camel clutch and his manager Abdullah Farouk, who was always sneaking foreign objects into the ring for the Sheik to use on his opponents. There was also Gene Kiniski and the great Angelo Mosca, who both got in the ring to make a couple of extra bucks between CFL football seasons as defensive tackle for the Hamilton Tiger Cats. Yvon Robert, Mad Dog Vachon, Chief Don Eagle and Brute Bernard, to name a few more of Wren's assailants.

One Sunday afternoon Wren left his house, got on the Upper Gage bus and headed down to the Hamilton Forum for his weekly beating. I was six years old watching the local television channel CHCH's *Maple Leaf Wrestling* as Wren jumped into the ring with Yukon Eric. Before the bell, Wren lost his shit and blindsided his unsuspecting opponent, putting Yukon Eric into a headlock and trying to poke his eyes out, right there, in fuzzy black and white on my TV screen.

A mob of refs and cops jumped into the ring to pull him off Yukon, and as the cameras pulled away to a commercial, I sat there on my living room floor in shock. Wren got kicked out of professional wrestling that day and then became the janitor at my public school.

From the hallway, my desk was moved inside the principal's office and it stayed there for the rest of the year, putting an end to my underworld adventures. But I still spent most of my time dreaming up new identities and tall tales. I shook off the obvious facts and took on the stories that most suited me. I was like an addict. I shot myself up with fantasy to make myself feel better and lose touch with everything real.

There . . . that's better. . . .

LAND OF THE LIVING

FIRST RECORDS

In the 1960s and early 1970s, Upper Gage and Fennell Square was a hub of activity on that part of the East Mountain. The Dominion store, Reitmans ladies wear, the LCBO, Woolworth's, Brewers Retail and the hardware store were all housed in an L-shaped strip mall. Sometimes Bunny would pick me up from school and take me to the Woolworth's lunch counter for a braised hot dog and Orange Crush while she picked up a bottle of Canadian Club for George at the liquor store. Across the street was the Busy Bee shopping centre. Bunny would never shop there because she thought it was cheap and that shopping there would make her look cheap. The Busy Bee parking lot was bleak and empty most of the time. The cars parked there were beaten up, and the people getting out of the cars seemed poor and sad. Mind you, we were some pretty poor, sad people ourselves. We didn't own a car beaten up or otherwise. In the late 1960s, Bunny found an Austin Mini she decided to learn how to drive. She drove without a licence for a couple of years before she felt her skills were sharp enough to take the test. But before that we walked everywhere we had to go. Bunny and I would carry paper grocery bags home from Dominion, and one always ripped apart, spilling cans of food all over Upper Gage Avenue. I remember Bunny once dropping a forty-ounce bottle of Canadian Club on the sidewalk. The bottle smashed in the bag and whisky poured all over the curb. Bunny broke down and cried, devastated because she had pinched the Queen off the bills for weeks to save up for that bottle. She looked down at me and yelled, "Shit, oh shit! Look at that, Tommy." She told me to say nothing about the lost bottle of booze, and she never told George about it either. She walked back to the liquor store and grabbed another bottle and threw herself at the mercy of the guy behind the counter. He knew her well enough to give her credit until she could pay the store back.

Sometimes we'd pull a wooden Express wagon to assist with the load and we'd even bring Trixie along for the ride. We didn't have a washing machine, so we took our laundry over to the Fennell Square coin automat. I remember that I never felt embarrassed when kids from school stopped and looked in at me and laughed and made faces as I folded shirts and bedsheets. Fuck them, I thought. This was a happy time for us. The trip to Fennell Square was our pilgrimage. I was proud of Bunny and pleased that she needed my help. Bunny always appeared Montreal-crisp and well put together. Her ironed shirts and pencil skirts might have been a bit dated but she was always neat and presentable, like she was ready for a job interview or a visit from the Queen.

Bunny was always ready for a little shoplifting at the Woolworth's as well. She loved a five-finger discount, and kept that habit going well into her seventies. She'd steal a wide range of goods. She'd take belts off raincoats in case hers got lost or stolen. In fact, for someone who loved to steal, she had an intense fear of people stealing from her. She was always checking her purse for her wallet, for her keys and charge cards in case someone had reached a dirty hand in there while she was daydreaming on the bus as it glided down the Jolley Cut. She kept her cash, no matter how much or how little, in her bra at all times. She taught me to keep my money in my shoe, my wallet in my front pocket and any big bills hidden behind smaller ones.

She kept me as her silent witness to her minor thievery. When I was small, she'd take me down to Eaton's and sit me in a stall in the women's change room. She'd tell me to stay put as she went to pick out a fancy dress. She'd throw the dress on over her street clothes and look down to me for my opinion. I'd tell her she looked nice, and she'd go back out and search for a coat. Then a hat, earrings, maybe a watch and some shoes. Finally, she'd take my hand and we'd exit the front doors of Eaton's with Bunny wearing her brand-new wardrobe.

When I got older and into music, Bunny would skip up to the old Zellers department store on Upper Sherman and Mohawk Road and as a treat she'd pick me up some records she thought I'd like. One day I came through the door for lunch to find Bunny standing there in her apron, beaming, with her hands behind her back.

"Which hand?" she asked.

"Right," I said, playing along.

She took her arm from behind her back and revealed Black Sabbath's *Sabbath Bloody Sabbath*.

Surprises were rare in our house. "Wow. . . . Thanks, Ma," I said.

"Now the other hand!" she said, revealing the first Captain & Tennille album. Her choices didn't make any sense to me. The two albums and the artists had no business together.

On another occasion of this "Pick a Hand" game, Bunny revealed the unexpected pairing of Bob Dylan's *Blood on the Tracks* and Donny Osmond's *Alone Together*. I imagined her skulking into the Zellers record department, grabbing whatever she could out of the bin and running through the front door, across the parking lot, jumping into her Mini and speeding away . . .

Bunny's eclectic selections helped shape how I thought about music. She influenced my connection to music in other ways too. Our kitchen radio was often tuned to AM900 CHML and its weird mix of music, from Don Ho to Glen Campbell to Patti Page, Dean Martin and Johnny Cash and all the elevator intrumental versions of the fifties hit parade and in between.

When I was about ten I got pneumonia. I came out of a deadly fever to the sound of a transistor radio that Bunny had found for me and placed beside my pillow. As I opened my eyes "If You Could Read My Mind" by Gordon Lightfoot played quietly in my left ear. It's still my favourite song.

I absorbed music with a ferocious passion. Every minute of every day, I kept a transistor radio with me. Several times I was caught in class with the single earpiece stuck in my ear. The white cord was always a dead giveaway. As soon as I was home I'd stick on my headphones, drop the needle on a stolen record and get everything turned up really loud. I wanted to experience the spit on the mic and the sweat on the brow of the singers. In one step I would go from Willie P. Bennett's *Hobo's Taunt* to

Rocket to Russia by the Ramones. Music was total freedom. There were no rules. There was no one to tell me how to listen. No deep study, no professors, no experts. Just my own imagination.

I loved 45s. And I loved buying them at Bob Moody's Record Bar, a mom-and-pop shop that changed my life. They had all the hits off CKOC's Top 40 on display and a huge back catalogue at cut-rate prices. From Bob Moody's I purchased the magic of Tony Joe White's "Polk Salad Annie"; the drop of the needle, the end of Tony Joe's count in, ". . . fo (four)," and then the best downbeat recorded in the twentieth century. I also bought the Jackson 5's "I Want You Back" and the Band's "Up on Cripple Creek" backed with "Unfaithful Servant." And I remember buying their "Rag Mama Rag." I took it home and put it on right away. It sounded like the music was being reflected off a funhouse mirror. I thought I had it on at the wrong speed, but that was just the dirt they brought to those recordings. It was real Southern Ontario soul right there on my turntable. All white-man blues and trucker pills, long drives and late, late nights on a seven-inch piece of vinyl.

In 1969 I was just ten years old travelling in a white Austin Mini down the 401 with an older mum and a blind dad. I was an overweight kid in a lime-green bathing suit that was about two summers too tight for me. There was a smell in the air that I didn't recognize but I knew was coming my way and a taste that was forbidden but that I would digest for years to come. We were on our way to Port Dover on the shores of Lake Erie. We drove Upper James Street to Highway 6, over Highway 53, passing the A&W, the Red Barn, Tim Horton's donuts, P-Wee's pizzeria. We drove into the unknown world of beautiful downtown Caledonia and the Grand River, with its legacy of transporting goods and people as rich as the Mississippi's. It's said that the Grand River was cursed by a witch in Cayuga after the town had persecuted her. She promised that the area would cease to prosper and would fall into financial disarray. Shortly after, the railroads took over and the Grand River became an obsolete means of transportation.

On the south shore of the Grand River was a Six Nations reserve. Here the complexion of the land changed, the cars got older, a little rusty, and the women got more beautiful. Great musicians came off the reserve and travelled Highway 6 into towns like Hagersville, down to Turkey Point, Tillsonburg and tobacco country, but I didn't know any of them when I was ten, and we just drove by.

We continued on down to Lake Erie through Hagersville, Dogs Nest and Jarvis until the lift bridge to Port Dover opened its arms to the summer paradise of Hamiltonians, or more so, East Mountaineers. Crossing that bridge into Port Dover was almost like popping the cork off of a magic genie bottle. The girls all looked like Betty and Veronica from the *Archie* comics, or better still the centrefolds from my next-door neighbour's *Playboy* magazines, and they walked arm-in-arm with long-haired hippie boys past bearded Satan's Choice members gathering beside the midway, sucking on bottles of beer, smoking joints and lying in the sun, surrounded by the overwhelming sound of the Port Dover beach bumper cars, the roller coaster and bowling alley.

The Band, or the Hawks as they were known before 1968, did six nights in a row, all year long, up and down the 401 and above and below it too. To me they were the sound of Highway 6 South, Lake Erie, tobacco fields, migrant workers and the Summer Garden dance hall. The first sound of freedom.

FIRST GUITAR

Glen Grey was my grade-seven shop partner. His parents got him a carton of smokes for Christmas when everyone else got Hot Wheels and electric football games. Most importantly, Glen had a cheap Japanese knock-off of a Gibson Les Paul. It was black and it was deadly, like a whole pack of wolves with six strings. It drove me crazy how cool that guitar looked and how cool Glen looked playing it.

In grade seven Glen started a band with Bobby Little. They called it the Green Finger. Their backdrop was of course a giant green hand giving a green finger to the audience. Bobby was the singer and painted half his face green to go along with the band's colour scheme. They all looked like kids except for Glen, who already had full sideburns and long hair. He looked like he stepped off a Harley every morning before getting in line with the rest of us. Looking back now, I think Glen must have been at least seventeen or eighteen. I mean no one thirteen years old had sideburns except for the Italian and Portuguese kids, and no one thirteen years old carried himself like Glen. He was the star of the band and he didn't know it or care. I remember the Green Finger's Christmas concert set like it was yesterday.

"I'm Eighteen"

"Venus"

"Proud Mary"

"Be My Lover"

It happened fast in the Highview school gym, and even though I was not cool enough to hang out with the band, the ripple effect of their shitty, out-of-tune version of these songs changed my life.

Glen was inside a group of guys I had no business chumming around with, and I had no real interest in them except they all had electric guitars. I was standing on the fringe of their schoolyard conversations when I overhead them talking about Alice Cooper making an appearance on the debut episode of ABC TV's *In Concert*, November 24, 1972. Alice Cooper on TV? I'd only seen photos of him in magazines and on posters down at a head shop on King Street called This Is It.

ABC TV's *In Concert* was a special show for the time. It came on at 11:30 p.m., after the news. Its cameras went right into the concert halls, recording live performances when anything could happen. Lots did. I saw Billy Preston dropping f-bombs one time, and lots of stoner moments, drunken rants, musicians getting crap thrown at them on stage, people falling down and brawls in the audience. It was real, raw television viewing.

That first episode of the show featured Curtis Mayfield, Seals and Crofts, Bo Diddley and Jethro Tull, but it was Alice who kicked things off with a violent roar, swigging beer, throwing a trash can, wielding a switchblade. After that I spent a lot of time staring at the *Love It to Death* album cover, which featured Alice looking super cool, super freaky, and the rest of the band standing around wearing three-pick Gibson SGs, except Dennis Dunaway who had an SG bass. They looked like a street gang from outer space. Lipstick-smeared bikers or cowboys or futuristic mobsters. Dangerous as hell. And that's what we all wanted to be. Dangerous as hell with Gibson SGs hanging off our shoulders

"Chet Atkins introduces the Quick-Pickin' 'N Fun-Strummin' Home Guitar Course," was the advertisement Waddington's Music placed in the entertainment section of the *Hamilton Spectator*. The course came with an instruction record, a book and in-class teaching and—the clincher for me—Waddington's would hand out a "lender" guitar to anyone who signed up for Chet's guitar lessons.

I'd been on a long, painful road, watching, waiting, hoping for a magic moment when I could finally start banging away on some old plank. I couldn't ask Bunny and George to get me a guitar. They didn't have the money for that kind of thing and I didn't want to put them in the position of having to tell me so. But there it was. The ultimate goal. Advertised right there in the *Hamilton Spectator*. My chance at the only thing I thought about besides Amy Blacklock's ever-growing breasts and the mysteries inside the book *Chariots of the Gods*. I knew that if I only had a guitar I could do anything, go anywhere. A guitar was the rabbit hole that I could fall down and escape into another world.

I called Waddington's. The woman who answered explained that they took groups of twelve people into a class and introduced them to the Chet Atkins method. "Uh huh, oh yeah. And there's a guitar at the end of the lesson, right?" I asked.

"Yes," she told me, "If you sign up for the Chet Atkins lessons we give a home practice guitar to use while you are enrolled in the class."

"Do I get to take the guitar home that night?"

"Well, if you sign up, yes. All you have to do is give us a home address, phone number and show identification and you can take a guitar home," the Waddington's lady said. This was going to be easy.

"I'll be down there Wednesday night. My name is Greg Bayliss."

Greg Bayliss? Why of all names did I pick his?

Greg Bayliss was about four years older than me and lived on my street, though I rarely saw or spoke to him. It was presumed

up and down East 36th Street that Greg was one sandwich short
of a picnic. I just thought he was quiet, mysterious, like a unicorn
that just happened to live down by Queensdale Avenue. Greg had
been shipped out of Blessed Sacrament and off to Crestwood
Vocational School. Plenty of near geniuses were sent to that
school, and plenty emerged from its doors and into the work-
force as superstar tradesmen.

I went down to Mr. Walker's house, where Greg often hung
out fixing old cars in the driveway. I found him bent over the
open hood of a '71 Ford Maverick. I tapped him on the shoulder
and he turned around. "Hey Greg, how are ya?" I said.

"I'm good," he said and was about to turn around when I
blurted out, "Hey can I borrow your ID to go to buy smokes?"

"Sure," he said. "And while you're there, pick me up a pack
of Exports will ya?"

Shit . . .

I didn't have money for cigarettes. I'd have to go home and
scrounge around for change. I managed to put together enough
nickels and dimes to make up the forty cents I needed for a pack
of smokes. After I left Russell's Variety, I walked up Fennell, turned
down East 37th, the whole way thinking about how I could give
Greg his smokes without surrendering his birth certificate.

*I'll walk up the street and when I hit 36th and Brucedale, I'll
break into a run. I'll run, not walk, back up to Greg and hand—no,
toss—no, hand—hand him the smokes, run back down the street
telling him I'm late for dinner and I'll keep running down 36th
Street to Queensdale and catch the Upper Gage bus downtown.*

The no-plan plan worked. And I told myself that once I had
a guitar in my hands I'd slip back up the mountain, knock at
Greg's door and apologize about forgetting to hand him back
his birth certificate in the first place.

Waddington's was only a half a block from where the Upper Gage let me off in Gore Park. I was nervous and anxious, almost faint, actually, in anticipation of my scheme to rip off a guitar from Waddington's and Chet Atkins, whoever he was. I filled out the forms, offering up Greg Bayliss's ID and a fake address and phone number.

I was led up a side stairway and into a large room lit by naked light bulbs that revealed dirty walls and that hinted at a deep, dark Hamilton history. I thought of men's clubs, secret societies, white knights hanging around, planning and pacing across these old hardwood floors.

Waddington's was right next door to Treble Hall in a block of Renaissance Revival–style beauty, a gem in the heart of downtown. The corner building of the block, facing the intersection of King and John, has a giant neon sign burning out the letters PAGODA CHOP SUEY HOUSE. The sign is to downtown Hamilton what the Hollywood sign is to Hollywood, and that evening its super rays bounced off the neighbouring buildings and through the guitar classroom's filthy windows.

We all sat down on wooden chairs and a guy at the front of the room began talking too quietly to be heard by the three of us potential students. That's right, three. Not the maximum twelve. Three. He turned out the lights and started up a 16-millimetre film projector that sent a hum and grind around the room and a shiver up my spine. Onto the small screen came the country gentleman himself, Chet Atkins. Chet talked to us about guitar lessons and learning to read music, but really he could have been saying anything. He could have been cursing or talking backwards, and I would have just sat there, jiggling my leg and staring straight ahead into the darkness. I just wanted that guitar in my hands.

Bam. Lights go up and there's soft-talking guy and the lady from the cash downstairs holding three guitars out to us, and I nearly blacked out. When I walked around playing air guitar the moves I made felt natural. I couldn't believe how foreign the real thing felt in my arms. This was not my imagination anymore. This was guitar town, baby, and this moment felt like it was the beginning of the rest of my life.

FIRST BAND

In 1975 Neil Young's *Tonight's the Night* came out. After *Harvest*, after "Heart of Gold" and "Old Man," Neil said he had found himself in the middle of the road with his soft-soap imitators, so he steered his car off the road and headed for the ditch. He led with his heart and told the story of how it broke. The album spoke to me. It was filled with the excitement that comes when you take chances with music and don't care who or if anybody listens to it. I took one look at the cover of *Tonight's the Night*, dug into the back of George Wilson's closet and pulled out a ratty old sports coat, which after some bush parties, spilt beer and vomit, began to look like something Neil would wear while banging on his Les Paul, moaning and stomping through "Come On Baby Let's Go Downtown." I had arrived, but nobody was there to welcome me. I'd practise simple chords and changes on that stolen guitar until hard, gnarly calluses formed on my fingers. I borrowed music books from the library to learn Gordon Lightfoot and Bob Dylan songs.

My world was looking the other way. Disco had taken over. People dressed for school like they were stepping out on the town. Everybody looked like Tony Manero and Stephanie Mangano from *Saturday Night Fever*. I was out of there. Way out there. And I thought I wore out there rather well.

That same year I got hooked into a church youth group because the smell of girls that filled the air of the church was too powerful for me to ignore. The group was called High C, as in high on Christ. I know, but what was a boy to do who couldn't afford to take a girl to a movie or buy her a pizza?

Looking back, I do remember that the Italian and Portuguese girls at the Catholic Youth Organization (CYO) seemed much more grown-up with their more womanly bodies and mustachios. They walked the streets in their school uniforms with their beautiful smiles and tight white shirts and short kilts. But Bunny had sworn off the Catholic Church so I was not allowed through the doors of that swinging CYO scene. Instead, I wandered into the white world of the United Church to find a girl, any girl, to bring out the poet in me.

It was at one of these High C gatherings that a counsellor named Ken Keith pulled out a guitar and started playing Jim Croce songs and a few Christian diddies like "This Little Light of Mine." I didn't pay much attention to the music, but I did notice how the girls, exhausted from all the Jesus talk and the heat coming off the electric radiators in the small, modern chapel, looked suddenly hopeful, as if this guy in a powder-blue leisure suit with an Ovation guitar might just save them from death by boredom.

After that Sunday I signed myself into the music department at my high school. I had no interest in joining the school band. I didn't even have an interest in showing up to class or reading music. All I was focused on were the two upright basses that the music department owned. I'd been listening to the album *Will the Circle Be Unbroken*, a collection of beautiful white-man blues, country, Appalachian folk and bluegrass music the Nitty Gritty Dirt Band recorded with the godfathers, grand-fathers and legends—Roy Acuff, "Mother" Maybelle Carter, Doc Watson, Earl Scruggs, Merle Travis and Jimmy Martin. Listening to this record, studying the liner notes and staring at the pictures on the three-album set, I discovered the playing of Junior Huskey. He was the guy with the out-of-fashion black-rimmed glasses and short, Southern-looking haircut whose bass playing put the heart-beat into the songs on that record. Junior Huskey was the reason I wanted to play the upright bass, and why I was in music class at all. I eyed those two basses, and when my chance came I carried one of them from the instrument holding room and out the auditorium loading door. I held on to it for the rest of my time in high school.

Meanwhile, back at High C, Ken Keith was still playing Jim Croce and Cat Stevens in between the usual white-bread god songs. Ken was older, in teachers' college and dying to get in front of an audience to do his thing. He'd grown up performing as the sidekick to Rollo the Clown, his father, who was also a church elder and a car salesman. When Ken found out that I had an upright bass hiding in my bedroom, he asked me if I could play. I said sure. He said, "Bring it in to High C. Let's play." And that was that.

We started playing a "folk mass" at church. We played "Rise and Shine and Give God the Glory Glory." Hands were clapping and my bass strings were thumping, and my feet left the altar. I looked over the heads of the congregation, over the circus and the sewer. I was free for the first time in that moment and nobody could bring me down off the ceiling. Well, nobody except Ken. After church we'd get together to play some more of his favourite John Denver tunes. Ken and I just weren't on the same frequency.

I'd been so moved by *Tonight's the Night* that I started writing songs as soon as I figured out a few more chords on my other stolen instrument, the Waddington's guitar. I was a crap guitar player and not a great singer, but when I sang my own words with my own chords, I could sing them whichever way I wanted. And if I messed up, then that was fine and dandy with me. I figured my songs might come in handy at the church group. I borrowed a twelve-string guitar from my neighbour Ricky Strang and played a couple of my originals—"Bad Time for Love" and "Music Man"—for the group. The next week Counsellor Ken returned with his own songs to play, including one called "Thanks for People." He had me learn that one and taught me the back-up vocals. My songs were immediately shelved, and it was all about "Thanks for People." I'd stand there beside him and sing "Awwwwweeeee aaaahhhhhch awwwweeee," and whisper the line, "thanks for people," behind him.

Each week Ken would come in with a whole new batch of pretty horrible songs that leaned on desperate, down-and-out characters and featured Ken as a godlike narrator. They were modern-day Bible stories for children, only with adult themes, like "Dark Lady," about a lady who does drugs and lives in a hotel room across the hall from god and dies. Then Ken decided we were going to put a band together, which is when I should have come right out and said no. But instead, like a guy who wants to break up with his girlfriend as she's moving into his apartment and unpacking her bags, I just let it all happen.

He came up with a few names, ran them by me and finally decided on Serenity. Serenity? What was happening to my life, I thought. By this time, I had Ricky Strang's twelve-string guitar on long-term loan. Ken got another guy to join the band who could not sing or play but who owned an electric guitar and small amp. Jim was even older than Ken and had a job as a junior exec at Procter & Gamble, so what he was doing in Serenity was beyond me.

Ken gave Jim one song to sing at every show. He always chose "Softly" by Gordon Lightfoot and dedicated it to his wife, who was never at any of our concerts. Well, they weren't really concerts. They were more like musical interludes, three or four songs performed at church services and functions like plays, picnics, bake sales and Boy Scout father–son banquets. (We did manage one concert at an old-folks home, but the staff thought Jim's five-watt amp was a little too loud for the seniors, so we never really finished that one.) Our audience at these interludes was most often made up of the High C's, who had to follow us around, and really old people, who had nothing else to do but sit there and nod off while hanging out at the church for whatever action there was to soak up. It was a safe gig. A horrible gig, but a safe one because no one would ever know what I was up to. Serenity was my super-secret life, a life that I led without consequence.

That is, until Ken came in one Sunday and told me he had booked a real gig for us. A real gig. For real money! "It pays fifty bucks," Ken said. "And get this, Tom—it's all going down in the cafeteria of your high school."

What?

I saw A Foot in Coldwater in an after-school concert in our auditorium. They had a massive hit on the radio called "Make Me Do Anything You Want." It was pretty impressive. I also saw Steel River play in our school gym. They had less of a hit on the radio called "Southbound Train." That was pretty impressive too. These bands were cool, and the guys in them long-haired, dirty bastards. They looked like guys you'd try to avoid if you ran into them downtown. But now Sherwood Secondary would be getting a taste of Serenity.

I wanted to die. My secret life was about to be revealed to the biggest group of assholes on the face of the earth: my friends. I closed my eyes and pictured Ken in his powder-blue leisure suit and Jim in his double knits throwing down some super-soft Christian out-of-tune folk-rock for the school I tried to avoid even when I was supposed to be there.

The night of the concert was a blur. I wore my Neil Young *Tonight's the Night* uniform in an attempt to bring some cool to the occasion, and then I got stoned. The concert went by fast, but not fast enough. I stood there with Ricky Strang's twelve-string guitar around my neck, staring out like a deer under the wheels of a transport truck. I was already dead as Ken made stupid jokes at my expense and told stories with moral endings about drugs and premarital sex. Looking out into the dark cafeteria, I saw the football team and the cheerleaders and my buddies from the smoking area and the Italian mobster kids in their Studio 54 disco getups and I sank into a deep depression. My legs were broken and my head was smashed just like the dead deer I was imagining in my stoned head. My life was over.

No one was ever going to buy weed off me again, and if they did, they'd complain about the count or the quality or the price. Even my buddies who blew stuff up in chemistry class knew how bad we were. When I walked into my home room the next morning, they were already laughing. Ted Clement stopped only for a second and only to squeeze out two words. "You suck."

My buddy Dave Cross agreed wholeheartedly. "Yeah, man. You were terrible. Just horrible."

I couldn't have picked a worse band to be in. I knew I had to move on.

FIRST TASTE OF ROCK AND ROLL

George's confectionery stand was in the post office at the corner of Main and John Street. Bunny helped out, filling in supply orders and making bank deposits a couple of times a week. I would hang around and watch George take cash and dole out cigarettes, candy bars, bags of chips and bottles of Coke and ginger ale. It was amazing to see a man with no sight run his hands across the inventory and grab the desired flavour of Hostess potato chips and the right pack of smokes, tossing them across the counter to his customers. Payment was handled through an honour system, of course, and reflected the respect people had for men who had sacrificed so much. It was easy for George to trust his patrons.

When I was thirteen, George was harassed and bullied by a group of punks who had no such regard. When they looked at George, they just saw an easy target. They mocked his blindness, slapped him around a bit, stole his money and all his boxes of cigarettes. And when he tried to defend himself with his wooden cane, they grabbed it from his hands and threw it down the hallway of the post office. They kept this up for a while, I guess, and they picked times when the place was fairly deserted. Fucking cowards.

I sat in George's chair in the living room, crying as I listened closely to George whispering the details of the attacks to Bunny in the kitchen. My spirits sank. George had been my very own war hero. I brought his medals to school for show and tell, and marvelled at his bloodied air force flight boots that were kept in his old RCAF bag in the basement. But the man I had proudly led through parades on Remembrance Day was again a fallen soldier, only this time I was there to hear every horrible detail.

I'm ashamed to admit that the day he came home battered up and scared was the day George stopped being my hero. He seemed small and weak to me, and I was washed over with feelings that bullied my childhood beliefs and pushed my heart so out of line that I just couldn't get it put back into place.

George was never the person I went to for advice. And the distance between us was only widened by Bunny's insistence on using George to make me feel guilty for my adolescent acts of rebellion and drunken stumbles. She'd pull me into the kitchen and ask, "What the hell is wrong with you? What would your father think about this? Your father lost his eyesight in the war for you. You can't embarrass him like this after all he's been through for you, after all he's sacrificed to give you a home, to give you a life."

Years later I wished he was more of a father or at least more of an authoritarian. I needed him to curb my wild nature and show me what was right and wrong. I needed a force to deal out the rules, but sadly George was not up to the task of taming a young man who was veering quickly off track. He and Bunny were old. They were tired. And the problems I would cause were beyond their comprehension.

There were wild men everywhere you looked in Hamilton in the seventies—blue-collar devils, like Peter Fonda's dim-witted cousins. Kind of handsome and really fucked up, with perfect hair, bruised knuckles and crooked noses. All of them looked desperate. The north-end monsters, the factories, were unavoidable; there was no way to outrun them. These wild men didn't know how to run, anyway. They were the guys you'd send over the hill first to get their heads blown off in a war. In Hamilton they turned up their amps and took the fight into the streets and the bars everywhere they went. Hamiltonians became known as fearless rounders—all the edges beaten off them, round and ready to roll.

I knew them only by their street names. Hubcap, Slash, Crash, Slash Booze, Heavy Kevi, Curse, Nightmare, Slim, the Chicken, the Cock, the Ditch Witch, Bucky, Ear Bone, Sticky Dore, the HHump, the Itch, Swing Out—they were the regulars, or at least the ones that were regularly talked about because they took the chances or had the drugs or just got out of jail or were going to court or got some shitty gig doing the fourth-set country and western matinee down on Barton Street at the Prince Edward Tavern, or an even shittier gig playing guitar for some band that did Doobie Brothers covers six nights a week in the east end somewhere. At least the Prince Edward Tavern gig offered a hot meal and a chance to play some great old Buck Owens and Lefty Frizzell songs

For musical inspiration, Hamilton looked towards Detroit, not Yonge Street. We ate up the Stooges, Alice Cooper and MC5 because we could figure out how to make that kind of noise. The city had its own overdriven, steel-on-steel matrix that affected our reality. The buzzing in the air drilled holes into the skulls of young men. Fellow Hamiltonian Daniel Lanois used to call this endless buzz the Hamilton guitar sound because no matter what electrical socket you plugged your amp into in Hamilton, you got the buzzzzz. It was like the industrial post-war knob-and-tube wiring that you couldn't get out of the walls. The wiring was already doing the job for us, creating our future. It was proof that we were alive, and it gave us the confidence to throw down harder than the next town. It was like getting into a cage with a drunk raccoon. You knew you were going to get hurt but you had to do it. We were falling out of broken homes. Not just the homes of parents who separated or divorced, but homes occupied by broken people. All of us were stepping out, looking for a bit of light, a bit of freedom.

At the same time, as the city's coffee houses were closing their doors, a place called the Pizza Patio opened down on King Street. It was situated in the old entrance to the Capitol Theatre. The grand venue had been torn down by a city hall full of assholes and turned into a parking lot and only the lobby remained intact among the burned-out storefronts, pawn shops and dive bars that littered the face of the downtown core. Pizza Patio was the only place my folkie heroes—Willie P. Bennett and David Wiffen and Brent Titcomb—had left to play. So I got myself a gig at the place. Six nights' worth. I put up posters and made some phone calls and filled the room with piss tanks and old pals. I made six hundred dollars playing there my first week. Six hundred dollars in 1976 was a hell of a lot of money for a broke seventeen-year-old kid with a guitar.

The gig went so well that the owner asked me back the next month. I took the offer and made nine hundred dollars. Back then, you could strike a deal to grab a percentage of the bar sales, and as long as the owner was honest (which he never was), you could walk away with a nice bonus. The next time in it was twelve hundred. I felt like a slut, but I liked the money and I got to play my songs, put on a show and get the stage time that I desperately needed. I knew I was doing the right thing but in the wrong place. I smoked a lot of dope back then and drank Brador malt liquor because it had a 6.2 percent alcohol content rather than the 5.0 in most other Canadian beers. The waitresses were pretty cute at the Pizza Patio too. They all wore these little off-the-shoulder kind of French-maid, kind of peasant outfits. Uniforms. It was an uncool gig to be sure, but the dope and the beer and the waitresses were all that counted for the time being.

I met a taxi driver who worked for the Veterans Taxi company. She picked me up at the Corktown bar one night and on the way home up the mountain we diverted the cab to an empty lot at the bottom of the Claremont access and we screwed in the back seat. She was thirty-three and I was seventeen, a perfect match. We started seeing each other most nights after the bars closed down. After her rush hour. She was the first person I'd met who knew who Bukowski was. That was a big deal for me at the time. No one at Sherwood Secondary read the same books I did. She also dressed like a man. Not like a hippie man, in jeans and T-shirts, but in button-up shirts with collars, black dress pants and police boots. And she drove a cab after dark all over Hamilton in the 1970s. The woman meant business. We never went to her house or apartment. We just parked the taxi along the edge of the mountain brow or down by the old TH&B railway yard or over at the Hamilton Brick Company by Gage Park and did our thing.

After a while she started asking if I had any friends who would like to join in with us. I said "What?" I told her no, I didn't have any friends. None. But I was intrigued. I thought that kind of thing only happened in skin flicks like the ones Sheldon Gunters's father kept in his basement wardrobe that Sheldon used to thread through his family's Super 8 projector. Blurry, faded, over-seen stag films for all us guys in high school to watch.

She showed up at the Pizza Patio early one night before I did my first set. She told me she was having a late-night party out at her house in Hagersville. She told me to bring some friends. I took her address and did my gig and asked this guy Ross Price if he wanted to go because I didn't drive and Ross did and he had a new Ford Mustang, so we'd be riding in style all the way down Highway 6. Ross hung around my shows eating pizza and drinking ginger ale. I'd see him out there. He was a fan. He should have been my first clue that my career was going nowhere.

Ross was a nice guy but he was even more uncool than I was. He wore double-knit pants and golf shirts with pens stuck in the pockets pulling the fabric out of shape. And often had on his head a big, fluffy toque. Like a girl's toque. I think he thought it was hip. I think he thought he looked like KC and the Sunshine Band or Sly Stone. But he didn't. Oh, and thick glasses. Of course he wore thick glasses. He used to get mugged all the time, robbed walking out of bars all over Hamilton. Poor guy. But he was a decent fella and I liked him.

He jumped at the chance to go to a party. I hooked him up with a Pizza Patio waitress and I asked one to come along as my date as well. So we all piled into his Ford Mustang. It had two leather bucket seats in the front and a back seat not worth mentioning. Ross got behind the wheel, and I put my date on my lap in the front passenger seat and Ross's date got stuffed sideways into the back. We roared up the mountain along Upper James, past Highway 53 and into the darkness of Highway 6.

The waitress on my lap was curvy. Sensuous. I put my nose in her hair. She smelled great. I was thinking about how quickly I could work my way through the party with her to find an empty room. One challenge would be my taxi driver. I sure didn't want her to get jealous or mad at me, and I didn't want to hurt her feelings either. The other challenge was that I was fairly polite and I felt obligated to hang around and meet people, to be gentlemanly to the other partygoers.

Ross pulled the car into a long driveway that led up to an old farmhouse. Some vibey music was shaking its windows, and as I got out of the car, I could hear chatter coming from inside

the house. My waitress pushed me up against the side of the
Mustang and started kissing me. We walked in the front door
and into a crowd of older people standing around, lining the
room. Ross still had his toque on, blowing our cover, so I separated myself from him for the time being.

I led my date through the crowded house into the kitchen and
poured her a big glass of booze. I told her I didn't know whose
house we were at, and I figured I'd act surprised if the hostess
approached us. I had two dates in one house at one party. I'd
never done anything like this before. Later in life, women would
be my downfall. Actually, too many women at one time would be
my downfall. I saw hope and beauty in all of them. They proved
that I was in the land of the living. On the planet. But as my
neighbour Mrs. Cannon used to say, "I can't tell the players without a program." This first time, though, I was just more proud
than anything else.

My date was secured in the kitchen with half a dirty glass
of pure booze. I excused myself and probably said something
stupid to her like, "Don't go away now." I headed down the
hallway to find the toilet, got in, closed and locked the door,
started to pee, reached in my coat pocket, pulled out a joint, lit
it up and settled into the moment. High. I fell into a dream and
came out of it with piss all over my shoes, my stage shoes, which
were Converse All-Stars. Canvas, so the pee was already soaked
into my socks. It's hard to be a Romeo with piss-soaked feet but
I figured I'd give it a try.

I flew out of the bathroom and wandered down the hallway,
following the music in the darkness. I thought I was heading
back to the kitchen, where I had left my date, but instead I was
walking back towards the bedroom. Fleetwood Mac was playing at mid-volume. The door was slightly ajar and I pushed it

open. The room was bathed in red light and full of people. Some shirtless, some standing in their underwear, all drinking and smoking, some giggling uncomfortably and others just taking pulls of their beers and staring straight ahead intently.

As I rounded the corner I saw the bed, and on the bed was this famous local artist I knew from around town, naked, with his head down between a woman's legs. As I got closer I could see the woman was none other than my taxi driver. The crowd around the bed were eager and excited. Another guy stripped off his underwear and stepped onto the bed, then a couple got brave and joined in. Pretty soon half the room was giving each other some kind of sex.

I kept my eye on the bed scene and felt my way along the wall and stopped. I looked away from the bed to get my bearings, and across the room, in the clothes closet, was Ross Price. I saw his groovy toque first, then his glasses. He was in there alone, eating a bowl of popcorn he'd picked up in the living room, laughing and watching the party-goers get it on.

Fucking Ross. I liked him even more in that moment. He was actually cooler than anyone else at that party. "C'mon, let's get out of here," I said from across the room, and he put the giant bowl of popcorn down and we headed for the door. We walked outside, I took the roach from my pocket and lit it up and we both started laughing. Laughing like we'd been in on some secret we weren't supposed to be in on. Laughing like you laugh at a teacher who has a weirdly shaped head or food in his beard.

We thought our dates would be long gone, but as we approached Ross's car we were surprised to see them, fast asleep in the front seats of the Mustang. We resumed our positions, quiet and passionless, and headed back down the mountain.

LIES

HUNGER

I never wanted to do anything else. I saw the Beatles on *The Ed Sullivan Show* when I was four, and yeah, I know you've heard that old tale before, but I was four years old and these guys were slick and had great hair and I liked their songs right away and girls were going crazy. I grabbed a broom out of the kitchen, stood in front of the TV set and joined the Beatles.

I grew up in a place where I was encouraged to do nothing— to stay put, stand still, not move, lie low. Nothing was expected of me out there in the world. It was the sixties. Kids still wanted to be cowboys. Men were going into space. Kids wanted to be astronauts. The Leafs won cups. Kids wanted to be George Armstrong and Terry Sawchuk. Not me. All I ever wanted to do was to write songs, play guitar and sing. That was it. That simple.

I entered adulthood unsure of who I was, where I belonged or where I came from, so I made up my story as I went along, and in that, music was my answer to everything. Rather than having the world tell me who I was, on stage, through my songs, I could tell the world. I was free there. No teachers to tell me how to do it. No cops to tell me not to. Just my own wits and guts to lead me. The path forward wasn't always an easy or straight one, but I was willing to do anything to find my way.

THE HAMILTON PSYCHIATRIC HOSPITAL

The Hamilton Psychiatric Hospital, or HPH as we all referred to it, was set at the top of west Hamilton Mountain on a lush green lawn surrounded by trees at one end and a sheer drop into the belly of the city over dragon limestone at the other. The hospital was perfectly situated for any poor under-medicated lost soul to stroll across the grounds, climb over a three-foot stone wall and jump off into a bloody, broken eternity.

I knew a bunch of guys who ended up in the hospital. They smoked too much dope and halfway through high school started to lose it. By the time they were of graduation age, they showed signs of high anxiety, manic behaviour and schizophrenia. My friend Harry made it through high school, but soon after that he climbed out of his parents' pool, went to his father's bedroom, grabbed the gun from the top drawer, walked out the front door onto Rendell Boulevard and turned left on Mountain Brow Boulevard. He went barefoot and still soaking wet down Concession Street and into the Royal Bank with the pistol shoved in his Speedo. He pulled it out, pointed it at a teller's head and ordered her to give him all the cash, which she did. Harry then jumped through a glass door and rolled onto the sidewalk. Cut and dizzy from his bank escape, he went up Mountain Park Avenue, over the jagged three-foot stone wall and leapt off the side of the escarpment into limestone, tree stumps and, luckily, mud. Still, he broke both ankles.

When the cops showed up at the Royal Bank, all the tellers had to do was point at the broken glass door and up to the brow, where the entire bank staff had watched Harry disappear over the edge. Harry entered the Barton Street jail, where he did the better part of a year before anyone noticed just how crazy he was and arrangements were made to have him carted back up the mountain to finish his time behind lock and key and lost inside a bottle of anti-psychotic medication at the HPH.

I ran into Harry and a couple more familiar faces when I took a little gig playing guitar and singing songs for twenty-five dollars every Wednesday to the droopy medicated eyelids of the criminally insane who were locked up for life in the HPH. The gig came my way via Bill Powell, who owned a three-storey house on Augusta Street, the first floor of which contained the Canvas Gallery with the Knight II Coffee House located on the second. The house was also home to Bill, his wife, Lynne, and their kids, Kim and Stefan. A palace of cable-knit sweaters and Earl Grey tea, it was also the headquarters for Festival of Friends, which happened every year down in the moneyed centre of the city on the wide green lawns of Gage Park.

Bill was always full of ideas, usually bad ideas that involved desperate young guys with acoustic guitars who would do anything to play in front of an audience. Besides running his giant festival, he also had handfuls of crappy gigs, from the African Lion Safari's food patio to the opening of a Burger King restaurant to

a ridiculous wandering minstrel show in the basement of the old
Eaton's department store.

I took them all, every single one of them. I even drove all the
way to Pittsburgh to play at the Three Rivers Arts Festival in a
tent full of deep fryers and drunk clowns making lame balloon
animals for kids who'd been towed down to the city's cultural
centre by their half-witted parents. For three days, I walked
around the tent with my guitar playing for people who obviously hated me. The deep fryers, the barbecues and the August
sun beating down on the tent got to me and I almost passed out
hourly. The extreme heat didn't seem to affect the drunken
clowns, but I guess I was just a little more delicate back then.

I wasn't the only one to take Bill's bait. Future members of
the Shakers, Dave DesRoches and Rick Andrew, and Fred
Eaglesmith took it too. Today Fred is as wily and gnarly and
successful as any independent businessman strumming a guitar
can be in this country. But back in the late seventies Fred was
just another guy who needed twenty-five bucks, and for some
reason getting locked behind barbed wire fences and steel doors
to go deep inside the hallways of the Hamilton Psychiatric
Hospital didn't seem to bother us. The gig may have scared off
many less-driven, soft-handed folkies for life, but not me and
Fred, and Bill knew it.

Getting thrown into a locked-down ward full of volatile
madmen and madwomen was one of those things I didn't notice
myself doing until way after the fact. I took my cues from Bill
Powell, who believed in me, but he was half-carney and half-
artist himself. He wanted to sell my act under the banner "Indian
Tom," with one, only one feather sticking out of the back of my
head. He had faith in music and culture and knew both were
desperately needed in Hamilton. Folk music, independent art

galleries. Long before Toronto turned its eyes towards us and decades before hipsters coined phrases like "art is the new steel," Bill was the guy who took chances when no one else would. But I took a look around town and saw there was nothing happening for me to latch on to, and nothing that wanted to latch on to me. I'd heard someone say once that you're not always born where you're supposed to be. I thought maybe that was my cosmic problem. I had to get out. George Thorogood put a song of mine on hold for his new album and my friend Bruce Cameron was living in Hollywood, so I saw an opportunity and went off to take on the world.

L . A .

Johnny Lee's "Looking for Love" was playing up and down Hollywood Boulevard day and night through every speaker, in front of every storefront and from the transistor radios and boom boxes held by lost souls wandering through time and space in L.A. The song was my soundtrack to failure.

Every morning I walked up Orchid Avenue and turned the corner towards the Howard Johnson's for breakfast. Breakfast was mostly coffee and toast and peanut butter. It wasn't that I couldn't make that at home. It was just that I needed to get out of the apartment to feel alive, and there's nothing that makes you feel more alive than being surrounded by death. I flew to L.A. in 1979 to give myself a bit of a change in scenery. I was reading Bukowski and listening to Tom Waits, and I knew Jim Morrison's ghost was somewhere around here too, probably roaming the parking lots with Bobby Fuller and Sal Mineo and maybe Gram Parsons. The place stank of people dying to be stars, and of others dying as stars. It was crazy town, a neon morgue. Disney-style tourist traps hadn't swooped in yet to clean up and take out the dead, so the stains were still on the bedsheets.

I was staying on Bruce's couch in the living room of his apartment on the corner of Orchid and Franklin, a block from Grauman's Chinese Theatre. Hollywood's famous Magic Castle (the most unusual private club in the world) was in one direction, and the wilderness beyond the red carpets in the other. The world of people who didn't quite make it.

I've often said I was in L.A. for months, but the fact of the matter is I went there to make a life and lasted about six weeks. I just couldn't crack it. I felt frozen stiff, as though the world was racing ahead of me and I couldn't get its attention. I remembered feeling this way when I was small and Bunny and George would shut down the house at five o'clock and go to bed. The world outside was alive, but I was dead, lying in bed like a prisoner as the summer sun went down. L.A. seemed to nail me to the floor in the same way.

The weeks went by and the money ran out until I was living off chilli dogs and playing my guitar for change in front of Grauman's Chinese Theatre. I was earning enough to get by, but not enough to get out of there. At night, I'd drink wine and watch the low-riders show off, see drug deals and fights played out under giant billboards of Olivia Newton-John and *Xanadu*. I'd end up back at the apartment wishing I could fly off the couch and through the ceiling, over the mountains and into the deep blue, straight north to Ontario and home to Hamilton.

The only music connection I had in town was a singer I knew from Canada named Bill Hughes. I had opened some shows for him at the Knight II Coffee House, and he was a vague but approachable way in. Bill was a gifted songwriter and high-tech acoustic guitar player. He was also the writer of a catchy Life Savers TV commercial jingle that sat on the tip of North Americans' tongues in the mid-seventies.

Bill had been in a band, Lazarus, who were signed to Bearsville Records and had lived in ultra-hippie Woodstock in the late sixties and early seventies. Rumour was they'd come up to Canada to do some gigs and stayed to avoid the Vietnam draft. They were managed by Albert Grossman, who also managed Bob Dylan, the Band and Janis Joplin, to name a few. I imagine the royalties for the Life Savers ad went into Grossman's pocket and up the Band's nose because Bill was not living the high life when I met him. Oh sure, Lazarus had a star quality that most coffee house performers in Canada lacked, but they were still hacking it out with the rest and the best of them.

I called Bill up and he was really cool. He'd been signed to Epic Records and was making a record for them, and he had a manager in L.A. He invited me out to play a few songs at a gig he had in a club on the Redondo Beach pier. He even got his manager to pick us up on Orchid Avenue. We all drove down to the gig in his manager's BMW, Bill and his manager lying back in the front seat lighting up joints and passing them back to me and Bruce.

Turns out Bill was playing in a cocktail bar with a tiny stage. He looked and sounded great up there, glasses tinkling and smoke everywhere. Bruce and I got up and played a few songs, but we sucked.

The best part of the night was the amount of hash Bill's manager had on him. Big cubes of the stuff, about half an ounce each. We all went out between sets to smoke under the pier, and during one of those breaks I asked him what a cube of his hash went for. I don't remember what he told me, but he did ask me if I'd be interested in selling some for him down in Hollywood. I had no money of course, but I convinced him to front me two of the cubes, promising I'd have the money back to him in a week. I told him I'd been playing for change on the boulevard and had got to know my clientele. Amazingly he said yes. Bam—I was in business.

I went from a hack with an old Yamaha guitar banging out Merle Haggard songs to an official Hollywood Boulevard drug dealer. I knew I had to stay cool though. I had to remain the pimple-faced kid out there busking for change if I wanted to blend in and keep out of the way of the other dealers.

I went back to the apartment and cut the hash up into ten-dollar quantities. I vowed I'd only work the trade during the daytime, high tourist flow. My little plan worked, and within the week I had the money back to Bill's manager and was picking up four more cubes to take back and sell. Within three weeks I saved enough money to buy an airline ticket home.

I landed at LAX unprepared, and I flew out of there a little more knowledgeable and a free man. I left my first love, folk, so that I could find an audience for my music. I stopped wearing my idols on my sleeve. I still loved Willie P. Bennett, Stan Rogers, Paul Langille and David Wiffen, but I traded them in for a Gretsch Nashville and a Fender amp. I kept writing folk music, but now it was loud. It got me an audience that was turned on and excited about music, and as a result I was excited about music again.

INSPIRATION

By the time I got home from L.A., it felt like everything had changed. Two months had gone by in Hollywood, but it seemed like years had passed back home. Dave DesRoches and Rick Andrew had been opening shows for Teenage Head in the late seventies, and while I was away selling hash and eating chilli dogs on Hollywood Boulevard, they were busy writing amazing songs and putting together the Shakers, a band that would flatten all bands that got in their way.

Dave DesRoches became Dave Rave, and as the Shakers, he and Rick Andrew hit their stride, and fast. They had lots of stage time as an acoustic duo, but coffee houses didn't know what to make of them. They played songs like "Poison Ivy" by the Coasters and "A Shot of Rhythm and Blues" by Arthur Alexander, and their original songs didn't have any obvious reminders of Dylan, Cohen or Joni Mitchell. The folkies hated them, just as they hated Fred Eaglesmith and me. It's no wonder Dave and Rick went in front of punk and rock-and-roll audiences, who were more open-minded and confident about their music tastes.

Dave's cousin Claude was recruited to play drums, and Tim Gibbons to play guitar. Tim's parents had come to Hamilton from Newfoundland, met each other at an East Coaster social and settled about seven blocks from Bunny and George's place. Big Bill Gibbons's roots were country music and the whole family loved it. They once went to see Hank Snow at the Hamilton Forum and the public address system broke down. "No mics, no speakers," said Bill Gibbons, "but you could hear Hank Snow clear as a bell." Tim had great taste and genius instincts about what to preach on and what to leave behind. I filled napkins in diners with things he said that I later put into songs, and he didn't think twice about the great one-line poems he shot across the table while devouring bacon and eggs. Dave Rave and Tim Gibbons were dreamers, and their music made every fibre of my being come alive.

THE FLORIDA RAZORS

We were all just kids, but my band the Florida Razors may have been just a bit older than the rest of the pack. I was the proper age to be in the knuckle-headed trenches of 1981, but the rest of the band flew in from different planets and time warps.

Carl Keesee was a bass player from Oklahoma. An American who came to Canada for a gig and never went home, he was like an exotic desert creature you'd find on the side of the road. There was no one like him around town, and no one who could play the bass as well as him. He was in Lazarus with Bill Hughes, so had the Life Savers success as well. I met Jason Avery at the Knight II Coffee House. He was a folkie guy who loved country music and the French gypsy jazz of Django Reinhardt—which was not on the listening list for most punk bands around town. He played every note loud and with unexpected phrasings. His guitar solos made our audiences dance like they were auditioning for parts in a shaky pre-war cartoon. Greg Cannon was from the East Mountain. He was a total rounder and looked like an ex–speed freak, but his claim to fame was having played in a popular local band called Buxton Castle. He wore that era head to toe: handlebar moustache, long dirty-blond hair, bell bottoms, and platform shoes that he'd strut around in to give himself extra height. He hit his drums like they were running away on him. He was a monster.

We were from Hamilton: we were nuts and our options were limited, so we played rock and roll because it was all we had and it was all that made sense to us. I think all those young fellas like the Tragically Hip who came to see us sensed we meant business and that's what they loved about us. They sensed guts. They felt the fear and excitement of Hamilton. There was a danger in what was coming out of Steeltown.

Teenage Head marched into Toronto and made off with the whole scene for the same reason. While most Toronto punk bands were posing with guitars and safety pins through their noses, Teenage Head was in the basement practising, getting it right so that when Gord Lewis turned up his Marshall amp, the sound that came out was like nothing else north of Johnny Ramone.

I had no idea what we were doing. I just wanted to play in a band that could play fast and loud and without apologies. We strayed off the beaten path and brought our frantic rock and roll to the draft room, Legion Hall and tobacco-country hotel circuit of Highway 6. It was tough down there, and if you didn't want to get a screwdriver in your ear or a fist up your arse, you'd better think fast and play faster. So we did.

We rode the 401 from Detroit to Montreal playing every hole and Queen's Hotel we could find. We hit town in those days with the intent to survive, and I had a "to-do list" of mental and physical chores that had to be executed to keep us in tip-top shape and keep the wheels on the road financially. Because we played six nights a week in the same spot, and played three or four shows a night, we lived upstairs above the bar. We felt right at home to run up a mighty bar tab, stole food from the kitchen after hours to cook on a hotplate we carried with us, sold weed and speed to the patrons under the nose of the local dealers, partied with the locals after hours, screwed the waitresses, got in fist fights with owners, waited for the cash—no cheques ever—and on Saturday night, we got the hell out of there.

You do stupid things, when you're hungry.

THE HONEYED CENTRE

Looking back, it seems impossible that we were ever that young. I was twenty-four, she was twenty-three. We seemed so old at the time.

I was with the Florida Razors in Kingston for a week after doing shows in Detroit, London and Trenton, Ontario. The gig in Trenton had been a low point. We played at the Sherwood Forest Inn for six demoralizing nights, going on between stripper shows during the day, and at night performing three forty-five-minute sets. The place was so bad that all the strippers quit except for one, and I ended up sleeping with her. She looked like Liza Minnelli from *Cabaret*. Well, not quite.

Sandy was waitressing at the Prince George Hotel in Kingston, and was wearing what I would later refer to as her Barbarella dress—it was black and tight and had two holes cut into the sides revealing wide-open flesh. Sandy slid over to the table I was sitting at between sets. I think she thought I was some kind of badass, which was not at all true. I felt more like the Johnny Cash line, "Made up of bad parts, but trying to do good."

Something like that.

We made an impression on one another, and a couple of nights later I watched her serving tables through a window from the bar next door as the radio played Elton John's "I Guess That's Why They Call It the Blues" and Madonna's "Borderline." Two songs I still can't hear without thinking immediately of the moment and that crazy dress.

Somehow we ended up sitting on the couch in Sandy's rooming house, smoking dope and laughing until the world turned blue. I wore an old trench coat that was too flimsy for the early winter freeze blowing off Lake Ontario. We went to breakfast at Morrison's Restaurant down on King Street. I sang Pablo Cruise songs into the sausage I had impaled on my fork. I looked across the table at her, and her eyes were laughing. I knew I had done something, something I couldn't take back.

It was November 30, 1983, and three years later to the day, Madeline would be born. That's some strange, beautiful magic.

Sandy and I had a romance on the streets of Kingston. It was a milk-faced little place where you couldn't go wrong if you came from money, had money or knew how to make it. The streets were packed with the privileged. The future bankers, politicians and engineers of Canada. All scrubbed clean and sent off to Queen's University. Sandy and I ran with the bikers and bartenders and waitresses and the invisible working dead that populated the nightlife of the town. We fell out of bars wrapped up in threadbare second-hand-store three-quarter-length coats, army boots, black eyes and hearts beating like Salvation Army marching drums. Dive bars, public houses, professor hangouts, the grad club, the Prince George Hotel, the Pilot House and the Old Royal Tavern—the haunts of that old piss tank and Indian killer Sir John A. Macdonald.

Sandy had it all. A cutting sense of humour, hair-trigger temper, raven-black hair, an intellect that stumped me most of the time. Our priorities were different but our passion was on even ground. Sandy brought out the poet in me. She was the queen of the slipstream, a force strong enough to pull me along behind her, almost.

When Sandy told me she was pregnant, I was still playing music, travelling from gig to gig. I was still making Hamilton my home. I was still in a permanent state of coming down and getting high and coming down. I would get up in the middle of the night and drive the 401 to Kingston, arriving by sunrise and parking outside Sandy's apartment. Sometimes she never knew I was there. I was lost.

A wild man was raging inside me. I overdosed, drove drunk, got in fights and took chances with my own life. I was punishing my baby with a fatherless existence before she was even born. I was trying to throw myself in the garbage, where I felt I belonged.

It would take Sandy years to teach me how to connect myself to the people who loved me. She stood by, she stayed strong, even though I rocked her ship with waves of stupidity. She was about to give birth and was living without a permanent home, surviving off the loving kindness of friends and strangers.

Madeline was born on November 30, 1986. I was on stage banging out shitty rock and roll at Call the Office in London, Ontario, when the bartender yelled through the crowd, "Hey, Tom! You're a dad!"

I was stunned. All the blood ran from my head and I just froze there on stage with my band. I held on to my old orange Gretsch and stared straight ahead into the smoky nothingness of the London barroom full of punters and hangers-on. I felt like the ten-year-old James Ellroy in the photo the *L.A. Times* took seconds after the LAPD told him his mother had been killed. I was in shock. Totally alone.

It took me twenty-four hours to make the six-hour drive to Kingston. I can't explain where that time went, why it took me so long to get to Sandy and our daughter. I can tell you, because years later Madeline would tell me in a way I had to hear, that every five minutes for those twenty-four hours Sandy would ask if I was there yet. When I finally did arrive and saw Madeline for the first time, I knew she was the best thing that had happened in my life. I didn't know how I would come through for her, but I knew sooner or later I would figure it out.

As it turned out, it was later.

It took me several months to raise enough money to feel safe bringing Sandy and Madeline to Hamilton so we could start our life together. I had a little operation going at Moondog's Record Bar on the third floor of the Gown & Gavel in Hess Village. I stayed open after hours serving bagels and coffee to the drunks, while selling drugs and skimming money off the till. The cops caught on to my dealings before the owners. On a quiet Sunday night they sent a plainclothes officer into Moondog's. The guy was a good actor. He played the only drunk in the room, and I was keeping my eye on him when he rolled up to the bar, leaned in to me real close and told me that I should stay away from the Gown next Saturday night. "We're coming to close ya down," he said, then staggered away to the door and down the stairs.

I took heed and stayed away, and sure enough the place got

raided. I had pulled anything suspicious out of there, so I remained clean except for a possible file on my comings and goings and ties to local coke dealers and a few spotty characters in the neighbourhood.

Madeline. My saviour. She and I were deep in each other's hearts even when we were three hundred miles apart. Sandy and I would split up for months at a time because we'd get in a fight, then a bigger fight and then one bigger than that, and I'd load up the van and go back to Hamilton, where I'd ache for Madeline.

Once, after one of those separations, I came back to Kingston to take another crack at making it work with Sandy. We'd agreed to meet on Princess Street. I was waiting at the corner by our friend Ann Marie Rousseau's Chinese Laundry Café. I could see them coming up the street from about a half a block away. Sandy rolled up to me with Madeline in the stroller. I looked at Sandy and then down at Madeline. As she looked up at me the late morning sun got in her eyes. She was squinting, trying to make out who was towering over her. She put her hand up over her eyes and saw it was me. Now I couldn't tell if she was smiling or still squinting. She held a few fingers in the air as if to say, "Just a minute." Then she spun around in her stroller and went digging through her blanket and the padding in the seat. A few seconds later she came up with a bagel in her hand. She reached out her arm to offer it to me, and stared up into my eyes like, "Here ya go, friend."

It was time to settle into some good old drudgery and elbow grease, a straight job, and Jim Pollock's Construction and Interiors was an easy gig to hitch onto. Old man Pollock had been known to hire local out-of-luck musicians as unskilled manual labourers, including Steve Mahon, Teenage Head's bass player, and local psycho country crooner Ralph Nicole, who both drove and unloaded cube trucks full of drywall. So I joined that rock-and-roll circus, and Sandy, Madeline and I moved into a third-floor walk-up at the corner of Garfield and Main.

Quietly, Madeline and I knew we were in this for life. No questions asked. I loved picking her up at daycare and bringing her home on the Main East bus. We'd walk up Sherman Avenue to King and cut across the traffic to the Apollo Restaurant, where I'd watch her eat scrambled eggs and french fries while I drank coffee or a beer if I had any extra cash. It was calm and almost too perfect.

I had a thirst for booze, and Sandy had itchy feet, so there was always conflict swirling around us. I'd get drunk and stay out all night, and Sandy would get jealous of women she suspected I was running around with, and sometimes she was right. So the hammer would swing, and I'd be out the door and down Garfield Street to live at Pat Gibbons's house, a place that had officially been named the House of Men by the local rounders. Pat had his broke-musician brother Tim living there, and Steve Mahon, who had just been thrown out by his wife. Except for Pat, none of us had any money. We'd save up and pitch in for cases of beer, and then we'd play hockey in the living room, watch the Leafs and listen to records. It was a land of broken toys with hair and body odour.

I stayed at the House of Men until Sandy cooled down and let me back in the apartment. But I just couldn't behave. I spent more money than I made, disappeared on Sandy for days, got drunk, got in dust-ups, never paid the bills. I was a problem.

It was mid-winter, late afternoon, it was dark and our arms were full of groceries as we all walked home in the snow and up the stairs to our apartment. Sandy turned the key and opened the apartment door, switched on the light and . . .

nothing. No lights. No electricity. She turned around and sneered, not even bothering to ask if I had paid the bill. She put down her bags and walked straight into the darkness. I stayed outside in the hallway with Madeline because I knew what was coming. I heard her pick up the phone and start dialling the hydro company. Then I heard her scream bloody murder. I hadn't paid the phone bill either. We were stuck in the apartment with no lights, no phone, no stove and the food in the fridge heading bad. That was the routine. Fuck it, I thought. We have each other. We have beer. We're okay.

I never managed to pay the rent on time either. Our landlady had somehow lost a leg, maybe to cancer or a train mishap. I taught Madeline to listen for the sound she would make as she came up our stairs looking for rent. Madeline would hear the clunk, step, clunk, step, up to the second floor. She would grab her toys and we'd jump into bed and pull the covers over our heads and laugh. *Bang, bang, bang*, the landlady would beat away at the door, and we'd hear, "I know you're home, Mr. Wilson. I know you're in there. You owe me rent again and sure as hell you know I'll be back. . . ."

"Yeah that's right, you old cow," I'd think. "And Madeline and I will be waiting here ready for ya too." Then the landlady would hobble back down the stairs and Madeline would play with her Barbies and I would imitate the wind for her, and we would fall into a nap.

DEATH OF A WARRIOR—ONE

On a Sunday night in 1984, having been on the road for a while, I rolled off the 403 into Hamilton, crawled up the Jolley Cut, along Concession and home to George and Bunny's apartment on Ben Lomond Place. When I opened the apartment door, Bunny was waiting in her apron and looked tired and upset. I got the impression she'd been waiting there for a while.

George was becoming very forgetful, losing interest in the news on the radio and his favourite TV programs, drifting off and changing subjects during simple conversations. They had been in Niagara Falls for the weekend, and George had struggled to remember where he was or how to get around the small hotel room.

Bunny always mapped out foreign territory for George by leading his hand along the walls, counting steps from one point to the next, directing him away from furniture that might be bumped into or knocked over along the way. But that weekend he couldn't follow Bunny's careful instructions or remember the map. He had no idea where he was and kept asking her to go get Bunny. When she told him that she was Bunny he became aggressive and called for his real wife.

George was falling down the long dark hole of Alzheimer's, and Bunny had just noticed. She was devastated and confused herself, and she was looking for someone to blame. But there was no one. Bunny was about to lose another piece of the man she loved.

It's one kind of misery to forget, to not know your loved ones or your surroundings, to lose your sense of time and space. But to lose all this and be blind too is a merciless torture for everyone.

Bunny spoon-fed George his meals. She kept watch over his every move, through every sleepless night. I watched them together and realized theirs was a true love story.

Bunny saw George for the first time across the floor of an armed forces dance just outside Montreal. He was wearing his uniform. She took one look at him, leaned over to her sister Doris and whispered, "There's the man I'm going to marry." And that was that.

They got married in a flurry, and then she watched him hop on a train at Montreal's Windsor Station with thousands of other Canadian Forces servicemen and disappear into war. She was there when he came home blinded, addicted to morphine. She sat beside him on barstools at the El Mocambo, carried him home to their apartment on Huron Street, and now, forty years later, was still front and centre to love him through his final battle with the son-of-a-bitch disease that steals you from yourself.

After a while Bunny couldn't deal with George at home. One day, I drove them to Sunnybrook Hospital in Toronto, where Bunny checked George into Warrior's Hall. Hospitals are horrible places to begin with, but this one was infused with all the sadness that comes with an unwelcome finale. Wheelchairs lined the hallways. There was no clean corner to stand in. There were no magic answers.

I wheeled George out of the elevator and down to the end of the hallway, and got him comfortable in his room. Bunny insisted on unpacking his things, organizing them in his closet and drawers. I watched her arrange what seemed like ancient artifacts in the bathroom's medicine cabinet. The razor George used when, as small child, I would stand watching him shave. George would pretend to put Aqua Velva on my face and I would use my Dennis the Menace razor beside him. Now Bunny shaved George every morning with George's same razor, and she'd brought a bottle of Aqua Velva too.

His leather winter hat and his boots were placed in the closet, but he wouldn't need them again. George Wilson wasn't going anywhere.

I wanted a drink. More, I just wanted to wash all this from my brain. I pushed away my selfishness and stood tall to support Bunny. She was acting like everything was all right and that this was all just temporary. I stayed true to the pretense. I would not betray the weakened fringes I saw all around her. I pretended her pain went unnoticed.

It was a game the two of us had perfected through a lifetime together. We might have folded. Kept each other company.

Consoled one another. But I was too scared and weak. And Bunny was just Bunny. Hard-shelled outside, soft centre, with a veil over the whole mess, disguising her every move.

I sat there with Bunny and George for hours before Bunny finally tore herself from his side and we left the ward and took the drive home to Hamilton. The next morning, though, Bunny was up and out the door, on the GO bus to Union Station, and then onto a subway all the way up to Davisville, then onto the Bayview Avenue bus that took her to Sunnybrook so she could feed George lunch.

This went on for four years. George was emptied out. Held upside down and all the contents shaken from his pockets. He sat outside his hospital room in a wheelchair, unidentified to the universe. Who he was had disappeared through a pinhole of light.

But maybe he had escaped. Maybe his shell, his skull, his arms and legs were stuck sitting in Warrior's Hall at Sunnybrook Hospital, but in his long-gone mind he was running along a beach somewhere, watching the sun set into an ocean. Or maybe he was back in Cookstown with his mom and dad, taking off across the fields on a tractor, or back in Ireland, skinning his knees in the Dublin streets.

I wondered how long he would hold on. No sight, no legs, no speech, and as deaf as you could get before turning to stone. Sometimes I'd pull up a wheelchair and sleep beside him. I didn't know what else to do.

I tried not to think about the two if us getting haircuts together at the Fennell Square barber shop when I was little, or about him laying out towels for us in the front yard to have snacks on. I didn't think about building blanket forts around him in his chair in the living room. I didn't think about him drinking rum and smoking Export Plains at the kitchen table, or whistling along with Don Messer or cursing Dave Hodge on *Hockey Night in Canada*. All that was gone for both of us. I shared the darkness in his head and the nothingness that he felt as I sat in the chair beside him drifting in and out of sleep.

And then on December 12, 1988, I got a call from Bunny telling me that I should come in right away. "Your father is dying."

In slow motion, I watched myself get out of bed, get dressed, find my car keys and head out the front door of our rundown house. I knew I should have been rushing, I knew George was dying. I saw the big flakes of snow falling and filling in any colour of the day with white, but I just could not adjust my speed. I brushed off my old Crown Victoria, backed out of the driveway and, without snow tires, skidded down Barnesdale Boulevard to King Street, turned left and headed through downtown Hamilton towards the 403.

Somewhere around Bay Street I spotted an old rounder I knew from the Horseshoe Tavern in Toronto. He was standing in the snow just off the curb, hitchhiking. I used to buy coke off him. He was living in Hamilton now, hanging around Hess Village, causing shit, playing in bands, screwing everyone's girlfriends, and he had recently developed a large, unhealthy appetite for heroin. He was mostly drunk whenever I saw him, which was weekly because I was causing my own shit around the village at the time and we'd bump into each other in the wee hours after the bars closed down. And there he stood with his thumb in the air in a snowstorm. George was dying, Bunny told me I needed to hurry. But I pulled over, rolled down my window and asked this ne'-er-do-well where he was heading. Turns out he'd had a cheque waiting for him at the Horseshoe for a year but he was now so broke he was finally going to pick it up. I told him to hop in, that I'd get him there.

Why did I do that?

Maybe I thought he was holding and he'd have a couple of lines to wake me up, help me face what waited for me at Warrior's Hall. Or maybe I just wanted to avoid the obvious face of death. Maybe I was scared. I don't know, but the guilt I hold in me for picking him up, dropping him off and getting to Sunnybrook forty-five minutes after George Wilson died will eat at me until the day I myself die.

LOST ALONG THE WAY

I spent most of the eighties riding the 401 playing rock and roll in punk bars, fern bars, draft rooms and tobacco-country hotels. I was still a joker, a fuck-up, but now I was a joker and a fuck-up with a daughter and a girlfriend. I had been working, delivering construction materials to sites in high-rise office towers and performing demolitions, then driving to the dump where the ground at my feet breathed, raising and lowering me like I was standing on the old dance floor at the Commodore Ballroom. It teeter-tottered the entire truck of garbage and blew toxic waste through little holes in the earth, puffs of stinking smoke and dust five or six feet high. It was very sci-fi. I dropped out of music except for a few bar gigs I did with an acoustic guitar and sometimes my best friend Ray Farrugia on a snare drum, just a way to make an extra fifty bucks here and there.

Growing up, I knew Ray Farrugia by reputation only as a scrapper and shit disturber up on the East Mountain. I used to see him from a safe distance downtown. He was skinny as hell with purple-tinted coke-bottle glasses and a giant head of black hair halfway down his back. I'd see him flying out of storefronts, walking out into traffic on King Street like he owned the road. Fearless. He was running around making the fur fly, picking up chicks, selling drugs or possibly stolen goods, getting out of moving cars like he didn't have time for them to come to a complete stop. In the early eighties, when I finally met Ray Farrugia, or Ray Curse as everyone called him from his time in the punk band Slander, we became instant best friends. We pooled our madness to form a bond of survival that has lasted ever since.

One night in 1989 I ran into Dan Lanois at a local artists' romp in a studio space above the old United Cigar Store at King and James. The party was hosted by Denise Lisson, who had arranged for lots of booze and records and great lighting, but Lanois walked in with guitars and some drumsticks and decided to give the local artists some unpretentious, down-home music to add to the evening's fare. I joined Tim Gibbons and Dave Rave and Lanois for a little kitchen table party in the middle of the room. It was a moment that made me want to leave my job at Pollock Interiors and play music again.

Dan Lanois had become record producer Daniel Lanois and left town, and was now responsible for massively popular records by Peter Gabriel and U2. Lanois was always a fashionable outsider. He and his brother, Bob, had killer wheels and a fancy house that hung off the side of Hamilton Mountain, overlooking the city and beyond. It was at that house on the brow and at their Grant Avenue Studio that Brian Eno and Lanois gave birth to ambient music. But Hamilton was nowhere near big enough for the Lanois brothers. I remember Bob standing on the front porch of Grant Avenue with a cigar in his mouth, pointing a make-believe rifle into the night sky and telling me to aim high. He practised what he preached, and so did Dan.

That night at the United Cigar Store, I felt the unity of the moment and the commitment to making something happen, and it was Lanois who created that feeling among us. We dropped our drunken egos and became all about the music and doing the most with the moment. We each took lead on a few songs. I did an old Florida Razors song, "Italian Sunglasses," and the Carl Perkins classic "Matchbox." Tim and Dave did a few old Shakers numbers, and Lanois sang a couple of tracks off his new album *Acadie*, "Jolie Louise" and "Under a Stormy Sky." I loved "Under a Stormy Sky." It told the story of Dan's mom, Jill, migrating from Quebec to Hamilton in the sixties, a reference to my hometown I knew would be heard around the world.

After our little concert, we were hanging around in a tiny closet area in the back drinking beer. Tim and Dave were asking about the place Dan was setting up in an old French general's house on Esplanade Street in New Orleans. I could imagine the smell of the food and the sounds of the accents and bands playing in the bars of the French Quarter. "Wow—that must be amazing, Dan," I said.

He turned, looked me in the eye and said, "Then you'll have to come down, Tom." I was knocked over. I didn't say a word, just looked back at him as he continued talking to Tim. But I knew in that instant what I was going to do.

The kitchen table approach let all the elements I love about music come to the surface. It was natural and unrehearsed, and the songs cut through the grease that drips out of the radio speakers. Music without ego that travels on the wings of tones, blues and greens. I found what I was looking for. I listened to and loved records like Muddy Waters's *Folk Singer*, Miles Davis's *Kind of Blue*, the Cowboy Junkies' *The Trinity Session* and Daniel Lanois's *Acadie*. I wanted to communicate in the language used on these records.

Later that year I got on a plane in Buffalo and flew down to New Orleans. I arrived unannounced at the Lanois house and the home of Kingsway Studios, on the edge of the French Quarter. I walked through the side door and my life opened up for me. I knew right away this place wasn't for me, but I did want to lasso the creative energy that was there.

The kitchen was the centre of the house. A long table running through it seemed like the meeting place for both inhabitants and visitors alike. Two sets of servants' stairs ran up the back of the house, a rude memory of where I was and what had gone on here over the years. Originally it had been two French townhouses, but the wall that separated them was brought down either by demolition or erosion, and the house was now one grand, mirrored image staring back into itself. A broken, high-pitched hum was ever present. It had a life of its own. A ghost, or time trails, captured forever within the walls of the house. Or maybe Lanois had dragged the buzzy Hamilton guitar sound down with him.

Malcolm Burn, another Canadian-born music producer, took me up a massive stairway that led to the identical left and right layouts of the bedrooms and inner servant passages routed behind the main walls, and showed me a bedroom where I could sleep. There was a worldly kindness I had not experienced before. It came by way of experience and travel and sticking to the task. A guy showing up unannounced from Canada didn't bother anyone.

Lanois and Malcolm called us "canoes": Canadians who
had set their course for the old mansion in the French Quarter.
This was a place where art came first, and I was welcome to join
in on whatever was being born here. The whole city had a musical pulse. Marching drums and gunshots and singers' voices
time-travelling up and down the corridors of the French Quarter.
The madness on the streets never stopped. It was all tits and bar
shots, slipping and slumming over the cobblestones.

Meanwhile the walls inside the Kingsway were whispering,
and the hum never stopped. I lay low, listening, trying to hear
beyond the crowds outside, beyond the swaying dresses, vomit
and booze. Lanois was starting rehearsals for his upcoming tour.
He had assembled a fantastic rhythm section—Daryl Johnston
and Ronald Jones—to join Malcolm Burn and himself. He
twisted the arrangements and brought them to the edge of the
stage, giving the songs new life. I loved how Dylan did that,
keeping the listener guessing, questioning what they were hear-
ing, throwing out art instead of repetition. Lanois asked me for
some suggestions for covers for his show, songs that represented
Canada. I thought Hank Snow's "I'm Moving On" was a good
idea, and a little Willie P. Bennett. He settled on the old Doc
Pomus and Mort Shuman number "Little Sister." He said it
reminded him of Hamilton and the bands that roamed the bars
there. Teenage Head, the Trouble Boys, Dave Rave—these were
the musicians that laid "Little Sister" at Lanois's feet.

As usual, Lanois wanted his own take on the song, and one
night after the band went home, he asked me to help him
rewrite a few verses. He wanted his version to burn a brand
into the side of the classic rock-and-roll song. I thought that
was interesting and bold, and I happily wrote a few verses
without thinking much of it. But what that little request did

was instill the confidence in me that I could write something that could make contact with listeners outside the borders of Hamilton.

Sometimes all a guy needs is a little push in the right direction. The lyrics I wrote were a good trade for me. Lanois got his own version of "Little Sister," and I got to go home knowing that what I had was worth something.

Back in Hamilton, Ray thought I needed a band that put the spotlight on my song writing. He was thinking the same way I was, so we started hanging around my kitchen table on Barnesdale after Sandy and Madeline had gone to bed, and we played the songs I'd been working on from my time in New Orleans. We liked what we were doing. Enough that we went out looking for players to join in. We called ourselves Junkhouse. First we found guitarist Dan Achen or Dan O as we called him. Back in the early eighties, Dan O had skipped out of his hometown, Regina, to dodge a huge drug bust. He got tipped off and knew it was going down. Someone was going to be left holding the bag, and it wasn't going to be him. He was young. He was the devil that would stay on the loose. Dan O was a live wire, making it all up as he went along—sometimes genius, sometimes stinking the joint out. But that's what I loved about him and his playing. Other musicians mocked him. When he, Ray and I were putting together Junkhouse, there was always some asshole in the crowd who thought I needed to be told to get rid of Dan O. But I never considered losing him. Ever.

New band members would come and go, mostly bass players. Some would complain about Dan O. Some were embarrassed to be seen on stage with us. But I knew there was something missing in their playing. There was no chance in the notes, no moral in the hymn, and most of all, no desperation.

Russell Wilson was the last piece of the Junkhouse puzzle. A living, breathing monster. A bass-playing giant with all the humour and rage of a cartoon genie, and the intensity we needed to push our limits. He took us from being just another band to being a wandering gang of wild men. We met Russell when we were playing at a bar up on the East Mountain that was owned by the Hells Angels. Russell was the bouncer. That's right, the bouncer.

There's an innocence that comes with growing up in Hamilton. That innocence is often mistaken for ignorance. We don't rely on other people's words to define who we are. We don't rely on movies and books to define our character because we're born with plenty of that. We're angels and devils and hard-nosed, blue-collar survivors.

I'm not worldly. I'm a home-towner. And I was in a band of outsiders.

We took it up the road to Toronto and landed on Queen Street, where we thought it might find an audience, but instead of finding ears we found empty rooms, night after night, and fast-tongued critics of our dreamy, acid-trip vibes. Basically, they hated us.

We kept going, refusing to give in. We knew what we were doing was good. But as time went on we got increasingly frustrated. We started drinking harder at the gigs, taking pills, turning up our amps, speeding up the tempos. Then we started getting into fights on stage. Sometimes we fought with the soundman or the club owner, sometimes with the audience. It was like some kind of Steeltown performance art, and the louder we got and the drunker we got, the more people started to come and check us out.

Soon we were playing every song on ten and smashing guitars and kicking over amps and basically causing shit, which was our natural state anyway. We strayed far away from our kitchen table, but we had record companies and the media knocking at our front door.

The little Junkhouse concept was put on the sidelines, and I found myself in a rock-and-roll band again. There was no sense in turning back.

FATHERS, SONS AND A LOST BOY AT LEAFS CAMP

Bunny had always told me, "If your father wasn't blind, he'd have left us long ago." As a little kid, I thought this was a bit dramatic, even for Bunny. Still, I imagine there were days when the thought of the life he had with me and Bunny being it for him must have been pretty demoralizing. Before he became lost in a pitch-black pit with a plate in his head, tapping his way through the world with a cane, he'd been quite an adventurer. According to Bunny, George was known for living life in the moment. As a young man he'd woken one morning at his parents' farm in Cookstown, Ontario, thrown his belongings into a burlap sack and got on a bus to Toronto, leaving home forever.

He hit the big city and settled into a rooming house shared by a handful of Toronto Maple Leafs, including all three members of "the kid line": Charlie Conacher, Harvey "Busher" Jackson and Joe Primeau. George kept company with the players. He and Charlie Conacher raised hell in the bars around Maple Leaf Gardens, and George was front and centre for all their home games. His blood ran blue with his love for the Leafs. He must have had the time of his life.

George pulled some pretty cool stunts in his time. He quit a well-paying suit-and-tie job at the Bank of Montreal in downtown Toronto so he could go prospecting in Northern Ontario. Sometime during his lunch break from the bank he'd decided he wanted to fight the wilderness, sleep in a tent, bake pies and live among the Indians. I guess he thought that taking the tail gunner position in a Lancaster bomber would be an adventure too.

George's life wasn't the one he'd imagined. But in fairness, neither was Bunny's. She hadn't planned on taking care of a blind husband. She wore the badge of sadness and war-bride pride as she looked out for George every day. She loved him deeply, but life had got the best of them both.

The summer of 1967, somehow Bunny had had enough of George, or George had had enough of Bunny. Either way, the two of them hit a breaking point in their marriage and decided they needed some time alone without me to sort things out. During a War Amps convention earlier that winter, Bunny had been walking through the lower level of the Royal York Hotel in Toronto. She ran into ex–Toronto Argos great Frank Stukus, who had a storefront promoting his business interests, including a hockey school in Fenelon Falls called Byrnell Manor Hockey Camp. He edged up to Bunny, introduced himself, and the two began chatting. Bunny was a sports nut, so after she'd finished quizzing him on his pair of 1937–1938 Grey Cup victories, he handed her a pamphlet for the hockey camp. Bunny was impressed and wondered if Byrnell Manor might be just the place for me to learn some discipline.

I am sure she was picturing a summer equivalent of a private school or a military academy, rather than the typical knuckle-headed *Lord of the Flies* jock camp Byrnell Manor turned out to be. Bunny loved the idea of the private school and believed its type of regimen was the answer to everything. I saw through the bullshit and saw only white snobs coming out of those types of asylums. I wanted nothing to do with any of it. But I was too young to have a say, so I was shipped off in a yellow school bus with a bunch of bow-tied, blazer-wearing kids from Toronto, Boston and Long Island, who were also getting shipped away by their parents.

Bunny was right about there being a lot of money roaming around Byrnell Manor, and my guess is that Frank Stukus gave her and George some kind of charity rate. I was hopeful about the hockey part, though. The Leafs had won the Cup that year, and I had watched all the games I could. I loved playing street hockey with the older kids in front of my house. But I'd never been on ice before. I didn't even own a pair of skates.

Bunny hadn't thought out this part of the camp either, and as a result packed me off to hockey school without any hockey-related attire. Instead, she loaded an assortment of bathing suits, towels, outerwear and a suit for church on Sundays into an old steamer trunk she had sitting in the basement and sent me on my way.

Everyone boarded the yellow school bus for the thirty-mile drive to Lindsay Arena, and I joined them wearing my sixties-style summer leisurewear. When we arrived at the arena, the kids gathered their hockey bags from the bus and headed inside, and although I'd never been in an arena before, I knew enough to follow the pack into one of the dressing rooms. It seemed everyone knew exactly what to do, pulling out their shoulder pads, shin pads, skates and sticks for the day ahead.

An older guy settled down the buzz in the room and explained that we were heading to the ice for a nice long skate around the rink so the coaches could assess our abilities and place us in groups according to our skills. The room emptied out and I followed along, unnoticed. As in, nobody noticed I was wearing a bathing suit, a Chiquita banana T-shirt, socks and sandals.

. A line of hockey players, of all ages and sizes, spilled onto the ice, and as they began circling the rink in their magic blades, I hopped onto the ice in my sandals and ran unsteadily across the blue line and then the red line and then the other blue line. I didn't have a stick and my feet froze within seconds, but I didn't let this stop me. As I slid across the faceoff circle, a tall man in a Toronto Maple Leafs sports jacket finally put me out of my misery.

"Hell, son—what are you doing? Where are your skates? Why are you in swimwear to play hockey?" His words were harsh and to the point, but his tone was soft and understanding.

"I don't have any of that stuff, sir."

"Okay, buddy, let's see what they have in the lost and found for you. My name is Allan Stanley."

Wow—this is amazing! I thought. I knew who he was. I'd seen him on TV every Saturday playing for the Leafs on *Hockey Night in Canada.*

I watched as he sifted through a box of discarded and forgotten hockey equipment, where he found a pair of gloves, shoulder pads and shin pads, along with old blue-and-white Leafs stockings and a sweater that was maroon and red (Bert Robinson, M.H.L. Detroit). He found me a pair of skates in the sharpening shack, then dressed me, tied my skates and sent me out onto the ice.

I often think of that day. I'm kind of proud of my eight-year-old self for not backing down from the challenge of going to a hockey school without skates or equipment. I figure I must have been dumb or had big old balls as a young boy, or maybe both. Whoever that guy was, I remember him, and his bravery.

Back home, Bunny and George figured things out. They decided they had nowhere else to go but to be with each other. They patched it up, and it stayed that way until George died.

When my own son was born in 1993, I took him everywhere I could. I wanted him to see and do things I'd never had the chance to do. I wanted him to see a hockey game at Maple Leaf Gardens before they shut the doors forever. I got him there. I got him on the players' bench too. I never dreamed of anything like that when I was a kid, so I made sure he didn't have to just dream about it.

He was named by his sister. Madeline thought Sandy had a baby bunny in her stomach. We didn't expect a boy. Sandy used to joke that I couldn't make boys, only girls, so we didn't prepare. We had girls' names picked out for the baby, but the only boy name was the one Madeline came up with for her much-anticipated baby bunny. So while I was holding Sandy's head in the delivery room, whispering that she was doing a great job and that everything would be okay soon, she pushed him out of her body and I put my hands out to greet him and noticed a penis. A baby boy. Ha, imagine that? I thought.

Thompson had arrived.

He was like Buddha when he was a baby. He still is. The calm in the middle of a family of tornadoes, hurricanes and earthquakes. He could cool us all down, remind us that there was another way of getting on. He was the only baby I've known who cried to get back into his own bed. In the middle of the night Sandy and I would move him from between us in our bed to his crib, where he'd immediately stop crying and go right to sleep.

I remember Tim Gibbons, who for a while showed up at our house every night around suppertime. Tim would knock on the door, walk in, grab a plate from the kitchen cupboard and sit down at the dinner table with us, praising the meal with "delish, delish" and "this food is amazing" and "another home run tonight, you guys—outta the park, man" and finally, "that was great—I'm stuffed. . . . Okay, see you guys later."

One dinnertime Tim walked through our front door and the entire household was in the front hall. Sandy and I were screaming at each other about something; Madeline had every book in the house off the shelves and stacked high at the front door, teetering on collapse as she built an apartment for her Barbies; the two matching Samoyeds or huskies or whatever they were, were barking and circling us, knocking things over; the food was burning on the stove; and there was probably an unattended bathtub about to overflow upstairs. But Thompson just sat there in his stroller with his hat and mitts on, quiet as could be, watching us all freak out. Tim said, "Look at this guy. Look at how calm he is. He's surrounded by a giant mess and he's just chillin', taking it all in." We all stopped in our tracks and looked down at him. Tim was dead on. Thompson was the guy with the only good idea in the room. The watcher with the right answer.

From the very start Thompson had a natural feel for music. When he was still a baby I'd come home from the recording studio in Toronto and pick him up out of bed, put him in his car seat in the back of my Crown Victoria and drive him around playing a cassette of what I'd just recorded. If he responded, if he rocked himself back and forth like a wild man, I knew we might have a hit of some kind on our hands. When he was four years old I gave him a harmonica to blow into. With me on guitar we'd play the usual kid favourites—"This Old Man," "She'll Be Coming 'Round the Mountain," "Old MacDonald"—after Sunday dinners and family gatherings. Our first public performance was for Thompson's kindergarten class.

I didn't want my kids to have to work as hard as I did. If they wanted to do something, I'd make sure they had a chance to do it. In Thompson's case, it was hockey. Every night after dinner the two of us would face off in the living room for a game. It was the highlight of the day for me, and it always ended in a fight. Dropping the gloves and wrestling down on the carpet. When I was away on the road he'd miss our nightly games, and eventually he'd have to attack his mother or his sister to get in his weekly fight quota. He was three or four when I put him into hockey school at the Coronation Rink in Westdale. I didn't want him to have to ask or beg to play. I didn't want him to have to jump through hoops for the simplest things, to have to figure it out on his own. And I sure didn't want him to have to wear socks, and sandals and swimwear to play hockey.

BUNNY WILSON AND DOCTOR GOD

Bunny Wilson was always there in my consciousness. Standing in her apron, thin grey hairs trying to escape the bun she had put them in that morning. Everything she did was always immediate and everything was often a disaster. She had jaw-dropping, quick-cutting opinions on neighbours, passers-by, the old, the young, the crippled and the blind. She was a Montreal tavern wisecracker and Catholic-guilt survivor, and her knee-jerk, sharp-tongued observations would leave all of us shaking our heads, hiding our faces and stifling laughter, floored in our disbelief that someone, anyone, her—Bunny—could mock the world so perfectly.

In this spirit, Bunny may have hinted at the fact that I had come from another planet, dropped out of the sky onto the small square of backyard, brown grass bordered by a paint-chipped, rotting white picket fence out behind 162 East 36th Street. She told me several times when I was just a preschooler that there were secrets about me that she would take to the grave, secrets that no one, including me, would ever hear.

And there were the turtles. Sometimes she'd buy a ceramic turtle, push it across the table towards me, and stare silently at me for a moment before telling me I came from "The Turtle Clan."

"Okay," I'd think. "What the hell does that mean?"

She changed character in these moments. Instead of being her usual high-strung, French-Canadian scalded-cat self, she would act embarrassed or humbled by what she was telling me. Her voice would drop into a lower, slower, more under-standing tone, but when I would try to push for an explanation she'd spring out of her kitchen chair and dash over to the sink, putting an end to the topic with something like, "I'm not the person to answer your questions."

"Well if she's not, then who is?" I'd think to myself.

Mysterious gifts were always coming my way. Gifts that didn't make any sense to me. Gifts that the other kids on the street were not getting, that's for sure. No white kid on the East Mountain received Canada Post parcels with sage and sweet grass, beaded buckskin jackets, handmade lacrosse sticks and Indian rubber balls.

Later on down the road, when Bunny was in her early eighties and I was in my late thirties, and cancer had gotten inside her body, I would drive Bunny up to the old Henderson Hospital, where she met with doctors and prepared for a hyster-ectomy. The Henderson Hospital on Concession Street, one of the three hospitals where Bunny said I was born.

Doctors were like gods to Bunny. In fact, they were more

like priests or shamans. Their words came directly through the clouds from the sky above, from the mouth of our Lord and Saviour. Bunny gave servant-like respect whenever she was in the presence of a doctor. It was at one of these meetings on the mount that Bunny had to answer a lengthy verbal questionnaire. The doctor was sitting on one side of the desk, Bunny on the other, and at Bunny's insistence I sat quietly in the corner, making myself as small and as close to invisible as I could.

The questions went on and on and on, with inquiries about Bunny's medical, family and sexual histories, all those x-rays she had back in the fifties for that rare skin outbreak. X-rays that, by the way, were a very odd choice for a doctor to order for a skin rash, but who was Bunny to challenge The Voice of God? Finally, the doctor gets to this question: "Mrs. Wilson, have you ever given birth?" And Bunny answers, "Oh no, doctor, I have not. . . . Never."

The doctor puts a check mark on his paper and makes a note, and there is this (and please excuse me for my choice of term here) PREGNANT SILENCE that fills the room. Bunny is sitting there transfixed by the doctor, and I'm sitting there transfixed by Bunny, waiting for I don't know what, and I can feel the panic growing inside of me, and I feel like I can't quite get my next breath, and I actually feel myself lifting off the chair and reaching my hand towards Bunny and the doctor like a ghost that has wandered off course, or maybe more like Isabella Rossellini in *Blue Velvet* when she's naked and messed up on Kyle MacLachlan's front lawn and she obviously shouldn't be there. That's where I was.

Naked and lost in another dimension and obviously in a place where I was not supposed to be, and yet somehow this was the moment of truth I had been waiting for all my life. I had just heard for the first time what it was that was wrong with me.

Why I felt so out of place all my life. There it was, spilling out
so easily from Bunny's mouth. Had Bunny ever given birth?

"Oh no, doctor, I have not. Never."

So now I'm standing and the only word I can muster drib-
bles out of my mouth, out of the dark corner of the doctor's
office, and that word is put out there in the form of a question,
and that question is "MOM?"

Bunny's head whips around towards me, and she responds
like greased lightning. "Tommy, not now. Can't you see I'm talking to the doctor?"

And that, folks, was that.

The moment of revelation passed by like so many other
moments of revelation had passed by for years and years, duti-
fully discarded. It was like Bunny was the wizard, instructing
me once again to pay no attention to the man behind the cur-
tain. I had no Toto to bark and yelp and bite at the wizard's
ankles. In that split second, I became the fool that I was asked
to be and played along with Bunny's lie to me and about me, the
secret she would take to her grave. That moment faded and in
the next we were all back in our roles of son and mother and
doctor, and like I said, that was that.

HITS AND MISSES

JUNKHOUSE

Coming of age as a musician in Hamilton, I had the good for-
tune of meeting Barbara Sedun. She worked at a Mr. Print-All
on Hughson Street near Gore Park in the city's downtown and
took pity on me and a bunch of the local bands, printing for free
our street posters for shows in Hamilton and beyond. The Florida
Razors, Teenage Head, the Shakers, the Trouble Boys all bene-
fited from her support. By the early nineties, Barbara had a job
at EMI Music Publishing, finding writers and acts for the label
to sign and develop. It was Barbara who introduced me to Mike
Roth, and in Mike I found a fellow outsider who understood me.

Bingo.

I gave Barbara a tape that my pal and CBC producer Bill Stunt
recorded. Bill had managed to get Junkhouse standing still in one

room, playing and hitting tape. It was a wonder, because what he didn't know was that we had driven up to Ottawa with nothing but gas money to get us there and back. We were staying illegally in an abandoned, bare-bones apartment. A friend had got a key to the place and had left it for us. There were no beds or chairs or tables or lamps—no electricity. Nothing was hooked up. Every night we'd sit on the dirty wall-to-wall carpet and get super stoned and fight with each other in the complete dark. Yelling and spitting, aggressively arguing about who knows what. We were idiots. Every morning we'd go to the studio closer to knuckles than chuckles.

Somehow Bill got us to calm down and focus long enough for a few takes of each song, and he made us sound like a combination of garage band and Mystery Machine. The tape caught Barbara's ear, but her boss at EMI didn't get it at all, so she sent the tape over to Sony, where Mike Roth was busy discovering and developing great Canadian bands. He called me up as soon as he'd finished listening to the tape.

The guy was a hustler, but wrote songs like he was shooting arrows. Fast and straight and true. We became friends somewhere within the first ten minutes of shaking hands, but I can't tell you exactly how or why. We were nothing alike. I sat on the couch in his office looking right at him, watched him sit there looking off into space. He was talking music and his favourite writers and singers. He put on Tom Waits's "Kentucky Avenue" and went into a trance. Our musical references didn't all line up together, but then he asked me if I liked Neil Young. "Damn right I do," I said, and he relaxed completely. He talked quietly but excitedly about Neil Young and about *Ambulance Blues* and *Tonight's the Night*. I think he was just relieved to finally have someone in the Sony building to talk to about Neil Young.

I can't remember when he handed me a publishing deal memo, but it was after several meetings. I started my act. I came into his office, silent, emotionless. I slouched down on his couch like I was bored out of my mind being there with him, then I complained about the deal he was offering. "I don't know how I'm going to make any money by signing this deal." So he kicked me out of the building.

I went home and thought about Mike. Of all the scamming industry types I was getting in with, he was the one who actually showed off his passion for music. So I called him up and said, "Okay, okay, let's forget about that thing the other day, and let's get to work." And we did. We'd get into screaming fights, and I'd often leave his office in dramatic frustration and anger. (I slammed his office door off its hinges once.) But he never backed down. He should have been in Junkhouse because he was always up for a fight.

Mike felt like I felt down on Queen Street. It was a fishbowl, a whole scene looking for a break, with hangers-on hanging on like bacteria culture blood samples. Junkhouse had to go there and play our asses off to get traction, but we didn't have to like it. We did meet some kindred spirits there and got some helping hands from the Skydiggers, Rheostatics and Andrew Cash. We shared the stage at Ultrasound Showbar, upstairs from X-Rays, with cool contenders like Ron Sexsmith, Headstones, Barenaked Ladies and Lori Yates. The place was managed and curated by Yvonne Matsell and co-owned by Dan Aykroyd and X-Ray MacRae, who was a Kingston boy and brought a welcoming air to the place. He and Aykroyd also brought star quality and a much-needed cowboy element to the street. The Rolling Stones gathered around the downstairs bar alongside VJs from MuchMusic. I was just happy to get Junkhouse a door deal on a Tuesday night and enough money in my pocket so we could all get a falafel at the Hasty Market after the show and gas in the car to get back to Hamilton. Junkhouse had a long shot and a short window to make everything fall into place. And for a while it all worked.

For the most part we were a bunch of guys who never imagined getting out of Hamilton. The best I figured I'd get was a 401 route—Detroit to Montreal and back again—that would take me to my grave. Like Ronnie Hawkins and the Hawks years before, I thought I'd be playing in every draft room and Legion across the bottom of Ontario, and nothing more. But that was not the divine plan for Junkhouse. For us three knuckleheads from Hamilton's East Mountain and one skinny redhead from Regina, the world was about to open up. After years of slogging it out, playing music to sell someone else's beer, we got a hit.

One afternoon while the band and producer Malcom Burn were in the studio doing overdubs, I wandered over to Mike's office. He played me two chords on the guitar, D and C. And he played them over and over again and chanted in a low tone that made it hard to tell what he was saying. He reminded me of the patients I used to perform for up at Hamilton Psychiatric Hospital. The ones whose medication had not quite kicked in, who rocked back and forth, muttering, waiting for some relief to come their way.

Mike played me what he had and said, "There, write the rest." The studio day turned into night without any change in the room lighting. The band was heading out for dinner. Gary Furniss, the studio engineer at that time, and Malcom Burn were joining them. I stayed behind. I wanted to work, not eat. I retired into one of Sony's boardrooms. I'd been writing a lot after hours, after the office staff and executives had disappeared home, and I found the spaces in the boardrooms liberating. The possibilities for something good to happen were better in a larger space, it seemed to me. I had room to walk around. Room to think. I could climb up on one of the giant boardroom tables, stand with my guitar and perform the new songs from a different perspective. I sat at the table and started playing the chords over and over again, building up a backing for the chant Mike had started. I saw no need for any other chords. Just the D and C would do. I started singing, "I've been wasted. . . . I've been drowned in your arms." I was writing a love song for my hometown as I sang, an east-end Steeltown love song for the woman who kicked ass and took names. I wrote "Out of My Head" in about as much time as it took to sing it back. When the band returned from dinner, I was ready to record. They knocked it out of the park. It was all done in two or three takes.

It's the song that changed our lives for a while, taking Junkhouse out of Hamilton and off the 401 circuit forever. It put us on tour for two years straight and almost killed us as a band and me as an individual. The song went on to hit number one in Europe, and the top ten in Canada and Australia. We boarded private jets and stepped onto stages with everyone from Bob Dylan to Green Day. We even played a castle in Scotland with Jeff Buckley and Oasis. Crazy times. Times that made us crazy.

In any situation, the more drugs there are, the lower the quality of life you end up living. The people that come hanging around, and there are plenty of them, are not interested in your well-being. They just want to get there, wherever there is. Into the mystery of the dressing room, bring you drugs and do the drugs with you. You end up like a frog in a saucepan of water. The heat gets turned up and you don't even notice you're turning into someone else's dinner.

Junkhouse got to the point where we were outnumbered. There were more strangers in our dressing rooms than there were band and crew members. Bikers, dealers, see-through women in dresses that seemed to fall off when they walked through the doors. All looking for something, and acting like that something was to hang off our belt buckles. We never had the egos to let our success spoil us. We were Hamilton guys. Nothing was ever expected, so everything that came our way was a delightful surprise.

We were soaring. We'd signed a giant American record deal. What we had all worked for. The pot of gold. The only problem was we were a bunch of ex-cons and thugs and the crimes committed were tied like bows, or rather nooses, around our necks. Believe it or not I was the only clean guy in the band. The rest of them had one long criminal record that no one at Sony was aware of or suspected, although they should have after taking one look at us. The list of offences delayed the band from getting into the States. It killed our momentum and marked the beginning of the end for Junkhouse.

We rode a bit of fame from 1994 to 1997, then I had to leave. The booze and drugs and women were even easier to come by once I had some gold and platinum records on my wall. Funny how that works. I felt like the silliness of rock and roll was going to kill me, and I was right.

I had worked like a dog to get to the point where I had songs on the radio. Hits, in fact. I'd turn on a TV in my hotel rooms around the globe and there I'd be on MTV, or MuchMusic back home in Canada. My career was going just all right, and as Bill Withers said, "When you get to all right, take a good look around and get used to it, because that may be as far as you're gonna go."

BLACKIE AND THE RODEO KINGS

I was drunk. It was November 1996 and it was damn cold already. I had to leave the Rank and File show at Lee's Palace early in order to catch the last bus back to Hamilton. I had the loosest feet in town, eating up the freedom I had established for myself with Sandy, who was back home with the kids well into a night's sleep. All together in one bed, no doubt. I still remember how that felt, stripping down and crawling under the blankets with Sandy and the babies all sprawled out sideways, arms and legs everywhere, snorting and spitting with mouths open . . . paradise.

I walked, stumbled, tripped and fell across Bloor Street and down Spadina Avenue, past many of my old haunts, including a rooming house I would hole up in for sex, boozing, laughs and sometimes brawls. It was a crash pad, lit by a dim, bulbed lamp on a dirty window ledge. The mattress was on the floor and the bathroom was down the hall, and the sound of footsteps from people constantly coming and going echoed into the room. Like Dylan Thomas in *Portrait of the Artist as a Young Dog*, I was gathering my research, loading my gun and waiting for the right time to fire.

It was romance at its highest high back then, and Sandy and I would spend a lot of time roaming downtown Toronto and playing out parts in our little movie. We'd drink at the Library Lounge upstairs at the Imperial Pub on Dundas, about a block east of Yonge Street. The bar served up quart bottles of beer to the patrons—guys with army and prison tattoos resting on arms that looked like they worked hard for a living—and a jazz jukebox played Django Reinhardt, Dizzy Gillespie, Ray Charles and Charlie Parker records. The place was way ahead of its time, without trying to be. It had an old-world hipness to it, hipness that punched you in the face and threw you down the stairs if you got out of line. We felt right at home there drinking Bushmills and making out all over the place.

I passed the old rooming house and kept heading south, past the El Mocambo. The Rolling Stones played there. That's what everyone used to say. Keith Richards got arrested the next day for heroin. Elvis Costello did two nights there right after *My Aim Is True* came out. Lots of people said that too. I think about the El Mocambo because I used to do six-nighters in the downstairs bar. I dug a trench there several times a year, and I loved being there because the El Mocambo was the place Bunny and George used to drink when he first returned from the war.

I was going to take the lakeshore bus, not the express. It stopped everywhere I never wanted to be. Mississauga. Oakville. Burlington. It took about two hours to get to Hamilton. No rush. I welcomed the darkness and the smell of beer and smokes and fast food. I loved watching the city go by. The crosses and the Ford plant. It was a ride I could have stayed on forever.

City to city
Dusk to dust
It's all in my head
Traffic and God and then we rot out in the sun
Lovers, shacks and prison yards
For the lonely ones

I arrived at the old Elizabeth Street terminal with time to spare. I used a pay phone to call my answering machine to pick up my messages. I heard Colin Linden's voice asking me to call him, and I did.

It was about 11:45 p.m. and Colin picked up immediately.

I first met Colin Linden standing in a field in Gage Park in Hamilton in 1977. It was at the Festival of Friends, and Colin and I were probably the youngest performers on the bill that year. Colin was seventeen years old and I must have been eighteen. We came from different places. I mean he was a genius and savant. A prodigy. A student of North American roots and blues music and the men and women who dedicated their lives to it. He was a master at a young age and he could switch to Texas blues, take you to Mississippi, or up north to Chicago with a ferocious intent that left the audience that afternoon spellbound. I believed Colin was the reincarnation of an African-American slave, that he escaped his chains and ran for his life through the night across the blackness of Mississippi. How else could he have such a deep love and understanding of what he was doing? How could his hands uncover the mysteries and pull back the strings with such passion?

Colin and Stephen Fearing were putting a Willie P. Bennett tribute band together and wanted me to be the third member. There was nothing to think about. I said, "Yes—of course. When do we record?" We made plans to get together and play some Willie songs over at the apartment of Colin and his wife, Janice Powers, to figure out what shape the record would take.

I don't think I actually met Stephen Fearing until he showed up from Vancouver at the studio to record. I did run into him once at the Railway Club in Vancouver, but I was three sheets to the wind and busy with a couple of blondes. We may have shaken hands minutes before I ended up on the floor under the table. Another time I said hello in passing while he was coming off a stage at Nathan Phillips Square in Toronto.

He was a master acoustic guitar player in the tradition of Richard Thompson and Bruce Cockburn, and he could sing. He had perfect pitch, tone and expression. A giant too. Tall, skinny Irish guy who could write heartbreakingly beautiful songs about the spirits on the high seas and about trains crossing Canada.

Colin had the best band in Canada, bar none. The band members stood head and shoulders above all of us, so I knew I was in for a treat. Johnny Dymond was on bass. Johnny played with k.d. lang. I saw him perform with her on *Saturday Night Live*. He was a skinny little fucker with a giant Fender Precision, and he owned the instrument. Gary Craig was on drums. He was a powerhouse, a machine—the best of the best at driving the bus down the road. And the one and only Richard Bell was on piano and organ. I used to stare at him on the back of Janis Joplin's *Pearl* album. He was the one standing on the left, leaning in and laughing like he'd just told himself the funniest joke. As a kid I was mesmerized by him and his playing on that record.

I was pumped. I had found inspiration watching Willie P. Bennett at the Knight II Coffee House. Willie's songs were tattooed on my tongue. As a kid of sixteen years old, I dreamt of being the hero in "White Line," a lonesome artist, standing on the road, alone in the cold. I had become what I'd wanted to become. I had asked the gods to deliver me there, and the gods had handed it to me.

At the legendary Grant Avenue Studio, we made that record in three or four sessions, which were some of the best of my life. Colin had a different producing style from what I was used to. Every note played somehow found its way onto the recording. You needed to be sure about the choices you were making there on the studio floor. Everyone had their eyes and ears wide open. Three or four takes and it was over. We'd move on to the next song. I loved it.

At the end of the sessions I said my goodbyes. I was heading off to Costa Rica to make a video for Junkhouse. I thought that was the last I'd see of Colin and Stephen for a while. I figured we'd run into one another down the road, backstage somewhere, and have a few laughs. Little did I know that twenty-one years later we'd have put in thousands of miles together and hours of stage time and have ten albums under our belts as Blackie and the Rodeo Kings.

Little did I know that, with them, I would step onto the stage and perform at the Grand Ole Opry, tour and become pals with Merle Haggard, be invited to sing with Buck Owens, catch the ears of Johnny Cash and duet with Emmylou Harris, Lucinda Williams and Rosanne Cash. That the show offers would come through the True North Records office in Toronto, and the guy answering the phone would be Bernie Finkelstein, the father of Canadian music and someone who took chances no one else in the country was willing to take. That we would be managed by Allen Moy, a master at keeping me just calm enough through some pretty hairy times, then and now. None of this was considered as I stepped into a taxi on Grant Avenue and headed to Pearson airport that night.

FINDING THE DITCH

I was living at the Inn on the Park, up on the corner of Leslie Street and Eglinton Avenue in the northeast end of Toronto. The area was considered the outreaches of the city when the hotel was built in the early sixties as an upscale suburban get-away, a resort and business stop that was perfect for celebrities and rock stars and their hangers-on. The Sony studios bordered on the hotel's lush grounds, so it was easy to check in to the hotel for the summer of 1999 and record in a small studio space that my publisher, Gary Furniss, had outfitted for me.

Glenn Gould had once lived in the hotel. He set up a piano and a little recording studio in a suite in the old tower. His spirit was everywhere in that place, representing a bygone era of polyester and suede, the sexual revolution, mad bastards in grey suits and hard liquor. He was not one of them. He was one of his own. But his ghost hung around the pool, where he appeared dressed in winter coat, scarf and boots, sitting on a chaise longue in the July heat. His loneliness owned the place. I could feel him down every hallway. He wouldn't share his genius with me or inspire me to create. Somehow the weight of his madness brought out my own madness and cued up my addictions. I had the means to get heroin and cocaine delivered directly to my hotel room by downtown dealers. I discovered that if you spend enough money, often enough, you can get people to drive anywhere for you, even North York.

I drank the mini bar and watched movies on the TV while chasing dragons and knocking back blow every night. I crashed around seven every morning. I wouldn't eat for days at a time and then would gorge myself with bad food. I gained fifty pounds in three months, and I had to go over to a Don Mills mall, where, without trying anything on, I bought myself some cheap suits to wear around the neighbourhood. The cuffs on the pants would hang over my boots, and the sleeves rode high on my forearms. Sometimes I would park my Crown Victoria over at Bob Bannerman's Chrysler/Dodge/Jeep dealership and drink wine and do lines of coke until the sun started to come up.

During those months at the Inn on the Park, I wrote and recorded thirty songs for *Planet Love*, an album I would later release. I would wake up in total ruin, throw on one of those ratboy cartoon suits I had acquired and cross the manicured lawns of the hotel grounds until I reached a hole I had made in a frost fence that led into a fire station parking lot, then through another hole in another frost fence on the other side and onto the grounds of Sony music.

I'd walk past the office windows of the marketing department, the radio department, the sales department, staggering along the length of the sprawling one-floor complex until I reached the president's office, where I would stand and look in at him through the window while he talked on the phone. I'd push my face against the glass and act out some ridiculous routine for him, crack him up and continue on to the front door, flash reception my security card and dive onto the couch in my studio. I'd go back to sleep until my recording engineer, Jeff Desil, arrived and turned up the work we had done the night before.

We'd spend the day overdubbing on the tracks, then by mid-afternoon we'd start writing another song. We were in the centre of a corporate environment but we had been given total freedom. Nobody told us what to do or when to do it. Somehow, through all my few hits and many misses, I had ended up in an amazing, leave-this-fucker-alone-and-let-him-do-what-he-does position. By nightfall all kinds of musicians would roll though the studio, as well as the inspirational company of drug dealers, bikers and wildly drunk women who'd dance on the coffee table in the middle of the studio when we hit on a groove that was agreeable.

I'm amazed at how invisible a suicide can be. It hides in plain sight. I should have been scared, but I wasn't. I was losing what I had worked so hard to get. Respect, love, money. It was all on the chopping block and the axe would come down soon.

I finally drove my life into the ditch at the end of 1999. I was out there touring solo for the most part and entertaining myself alone in my dressing room by killing the hospitality rider every night, the same hospitality rider that had been supplied for Junkhouse's eight band and crew members just a couple of years before. The same rider that contributed to the

destruction of a great rock-and-roll band. The same rider that
stopped the hits from getting written and turned the shows
from the spectacles they once were into drunken puddles of
piss and vomit. I walked backstage every night and was greeted
by a forty-ounce bottle of vodka, a forty-ounce bottle of single
malt scotch, two bottles of red wine, sixty bottles of beer
(thirty domestic and thirty imported) and a quarter ounce of
weed, as well as phone numbers for some local coke and speed
dealers. I had arrived.

I was out there jumping fences and screwing the breeze,
from tour to tour, month after month, and as the miles rolled
by, bit by bit I lost my footing in reality. I came off highways and
into the soft centres of towns, banging on my guitar, hissing
and moaning through giant speakers. I stumbled off stages,
drunk and raging and hiding in the soaking wet blues of the wee
hours. I'd just keep going, down strange streets back to my
hotel or tour bus where I'd lie and dream of finding a taxi to
take me to the airport and fly far away, once and for all, through
the dark sky and up through a hole and into the brightest light.
And I put my head back, and wished I was dead.

I was playing rock star, acting like I was in with Frank Sinatra
or the Faces or Oasis. But I wasn't even out there playing on any
heavy-duty wild rock tours. On the contrary, I was out there in
beautiful theatres playing proper concerts with Blackie and the
Rodeo Kings, Jann Arden, Chantal Kreviazuk, Ron Sexsmith,
David Gray, Colin James. I was up there on stage bloated and
sweating and cross-eyed, standing in front of well-heeled, sedate
music lovers.

I was doing stupid things like chopping off my hair with
room-service steak knives while standing in complete darkness
in my hotel room. I wore old fur coats I found beside Salvation

Army collection boxes and drove nails into the heels of my boots until my feet bled. I dyed my beard blond, coloured my cheeks with red magic marker and walked out on stage. I would stare down secretaries in the first couple of rows like I was a wild animal. They were just there to enjoy a show, to hear songs they had heard on the radio at work. They didn't come for a madman who crawled his way in from the alley behind the theatre and somehow ended up there in the spotlights.

I was a monster, and there was nobody to destroy me. No mob to storm my castle with pitchforks and pots and pans and fiery torches. No one brave enough to stop me from what I was doing. I was on my own and I think I may have wanted to die, but I was too afraid to just cut my wrists and I was too dramatic to let the pageantry of it all go unnoticed. So I just marched on. Standing in front of dressing room mirrors hating myself, talking to myself, cursing and threatening myself. "One day I'll have my death of you. I'll find you in the poets' graveyard and dig up what's left of you."

Madeline and Thompson were young then. I had wanted to be successful for them, to be a dad they could be proud of. Instead I had become a threat to their happiness and well-being. I was going to be the dad who died on them. Who didn't love them enough to save himself. The dad who was too lazy to swim to shore, or too far gone to jump through the flames in the burning building, pick them up and carry them to safety.

These were the days when Bunny and Janie lived on the first floor of our giant house at 82 Stanley. Sandy had made a home for us all. The first real home I'd ever known, but one way or another I pushed it all away. I wanted to be there when I wasn't, but when I got there I walked from room to room trying to get away from myself.

The possibility of a blissful family life was there. The kids would wake up every morning and go down to Bunny's kitchen in their pyjamas, and Bunny would make them toast and cereal and cups of tea. Sandy would get ready for work and I'd get dressed, and then Madeline would take off for Ryerson Middle School and I would walk Thompson up Locke Street to Allenby Elementary on Hunter.

Then I'd walk back home and clock in for a day in the darkness. I couldn't calm down. I should have had my head examined by a doctor, medicated. I should have taken the drive up the Queen Street hill to the Chedoke Hospital psych ward. Instead I drank and did blow and never looked anyone in the eye.

So there I was, driving at full speed over every goddamn bump and curb I could hit. Luckily I didn't roll that mess. It just went flying over the gravel into the ditch across a field, and I stopped somewhere out there in no man's land. Actually, where I stopped was at Sandy's feet on December 12, 1999.

I had returned from a tour, and Sandy and I were sharing a bath when she said a woman's name and asked me who she was. Turns out Sandy had been worried about how much cocaine I'd been doing. She had stolen my cellphone, checked my call history and written down a few names and numbers in the hope of tracking down my dealers. One name though had stood out in particular. "Oh she's just some hippie horoscope woman who's been doing my chart." She was a hippie horoscope woman but she had been doing more than my chart. Sandy had heard this line too many times before. It was a lie, and this time she knew it. I sat there still in the water. Frozen. Terrified.

I was about to start trying to lie my way out of this, but there was no way out. There had been so many strangers, women. Each one proved to me that I was part of the world somehow, that I was alive, that I was not a ghost. How could I explain that to Sandy? The woman I loved. The woman who had given me a chance at having a family. There was no lie even I could believe. No lie convincing enough, big enough to change the course of what was happening in front of me.

I looked down. Then, as I looked up, about to say who knows what, she began to scream. She was shrieking, howling, as if she were being clawed apart. It was not a sound I had heard before, but I knew what it was. It was the sound of her heart breaking.

"Please don't make me do this," I pleaded with Sandy as she sent me upstairs to say goodbye to the kids. It was the longest walk of my life.

We were meant to be heading out for a Christmas tree. Madeline, who always took care of her little brother, had dressed herself and Thompson in their winter coats and they had sat on the couch, like a couple of good angels, waiting for Sandy and me to catch up. To this day there is nothing that Sandy and I regret more than our children having to listen to their world come crashing down. When they'd heard what was going on between their parents, they had crept up to Madeline's room on the third floor, and that was where I was now heading, up past the landing, counting the last five steps to the top level of the house. As I rounded the corner Madeline looked at me like no one has ever looked at me, and in that instant I thought that she, Thompson and I were done. The air was poisonous. I was sure we were all suffocating together.

I entered the bedroom and just started repeating, "I'm sorry. . . . I'm so sorry, honey." Madeline's stone-cold eyes softened and her mood broke. She walked across her bedroom and put her arms around me. This was tragic. Like nothing else I'd felt in my life, and like nothing I've experienced since. "I'm sorry, honey." Thompson, taking his sister's lead, came over and hugged me too. From over my shoulder I could hear Sandy's voice, explaining, "Your father has to leave. Say goodbye to him. He's going away."

Now the kids were crying. I was crying. I said, "C'mon, Sandy. Let's cut this out." But there was none of that. She was done. She dragged me like a rag doll out of the bedroom, down the stairs and into Bunny and Janie's kitchen on the first floor. They had heard everything. I said sorry to them too.

In her way, Bunny loved Sandy like she was her own. Both women were strong, and each respected the other's strength. The first time they looked each other in the eye they decided right then and there that this better go well or the war would be lifelong and of epic proportions. Sandy and I were married in New Orleans while I was down there making a Junkhouse record at Daniel Lanois's Kingsway Studio in 1995.

I asked the studio engineer, Ethan Allen, to take me to the airport in one of Lanois's classic Lincoln Continentals, black with suicide doors, my dream car. The plan was to propose at the airport, go buy a couple of rings and then head straight to city hall to get hitched. When I arrived at the airport Sandy was nowhere to be found. It took an hour after her flight landed for her to get up to the luggage level of the airport, and when she finally did she was a bit tipsy and on the arm of a Delta Airlines pilot. *That's my girl*, I thought.

We did end up getting married in New Orleans, but it was Easter so we needed to wait until the following Tuesday. In the meantime, Sandy went wandering the streets of the French Quarter in her sundress, still a little drunk, I think.

The morning after our wedding I called Bunny. She was

excited. "Put Sandy on the phone," she said. I could hear Bunny's voice coming out of the phone against Sandy's ear. "Well, good morning, Mrs. Wilson."

Mrs. Wilson. It didn't take Bunny even a second to know just what to say. She wrapped it all up in a bow and tied it around the two of us. And now that ribbon lay in tatters. Sandy took my cellphone, threw it on the kitchen floor and smashed it into pieces. "There. Get out. You're leaving the way you came—with nothing, and that's what you deserve."

She walked me out towards the front door. I thought the whole time that she'd give in, that we'd go upstairs and start patching things up. But there wasn't a patch big enough for this. Nothing was big enough for this. I stepped out onto Stanley Street. Christmas lights were everywhere. The city was silent, insulated by the falling snow. I walked up Locke Street, past the West Town Bar & Grill. I looked through the window—rosy red faces all drunked up on horse-piss draft and grease. A horror. I got to a pay phone and called Ray.

SOBER TRUTHS

I didn't know what an intervention was, but I was about to find out. Gary Furniss, president of Sony Publishing, called and told me there were a few things we needed to talk about, so I got on a bus and headed to Toronto.

For three days I'd been sitting at Ray's house drinking beer and gin, snorting blow and trying to forget what had happened on Stanley Street. This was different from the other times I'd been tossed out. This time Sandy meant business. I was shaky, white and puffy. I was lost, but had no idea how lost.

It was all a bad, bad dream, and I hoped to stay medicated until I woke up. Then I'd take a deep breath, shake my head clear and walk back home to tell Sandy and the kids about the terrible nightmare I'd had.

In this messy haze, I started writing a song I would finish months later. A song called "The Truth." I was digging into the trauma and looking out from the hole:

Wake me up when it's over,
it's something I can't live through.
I'm starting my car
and I'm driving it right back to you.
It's been such a long time, strangers passing me by,
each face looking in at me, they don't ask me why.

When I got to the front door of Sony, the receptionist looked me up and down and told me straight out, "Tom, man—you look like total shit." She buzzed me in and I walked into Gary's office. He was behind his desk. I sat down in a chair across from him and said, "Gary . . . I fucked up." The words rolled out of my mouth, words I couldn't take back. Then, in walked Mike Roth, my friend and the man who'd given me a break, believed in me. President of Sony, Rick Camilleri, was next, closing the door behind him and taking a seat beside me.

"You've been doing a lot of drugs, Tom. Your drinking owns you and you've been running around on your wife," Mike said. "Now you have some decisions to make." I started to cry and tried to speak, but I wasn't making any sense. He told me to shut up.

"We've made arrangements for you in a rehab for drugs and alcohol. They've accepted you and they're ready to admit you now. You'll be in there for eight weeks. You have a choice: You can get in Gary's car right now and we'll drive you there and admit you. Or you leave here now and never come back. We'll have nothing to do with you from here on. It's up to you. What's it gonna be?"

"But what about Sandy and the kids?" I said. "Eight weeks? I'm going to miss Christmas."

"Sandy knows where you're going. She knows we've made these arrangements for you. Now, make your decision." These three guys were more than record executives; they were friends and they were giving me yet another shot.

"Okay . . . I'll go."

Gary stood up, grabbed his coat and disappeared out the door to get his car. I just sat there, broken again.

Gary pulled his car around to the front doors of the building. Rick wished me good luck. Mike walked alongside me and told me to get in the front seat, then took a seat in the back. We drove off, north up Leslie Street to the Don Valley Parkway. Gary stared straight ahead at the snowy road. Mike stared out his window. I stared out mine. Three men with nothing to say.

We arrived at the rehab hospital, and Gary and Mike walked me to admitting. The attendant came out to meet me and buzzed me through the security door. Mike and Gary watched me go, then turned and headed back to the car. It was snowing. Christmas was coming. I hoped the kids had a tree.

Inside rehab I was sent to an office where I was asked a long list of questions. The woman asking them could see I was too shaky to write for myself, so she handled that duty. She was exhausted or burned out. Either way, she had admitted one too many losers, and the sooner she got me out of her office the better. There were rules. Lots of them. The main one for now was that if I chose to leave, I would not be allowed to come back. The end of the line, I thought. I had nowhere to run. I felt relieved. For years I had wished that someone would put me in line. I had needed George to wind up and slap me across the head and tell me to get it together, and when I needed it the most, he couldn't do it. Finally, that slap I'd been waiting for had come.

The woman handed me a bottle of water and a cup containing two pills and told me to swallow them. I did. "I have to call home and let my wife know where I am," I said. She dialled the number for me and Sandy answered. I told her that I was going away for a while.

"I know," she said. "It's going to be okay."

"Is it? Is everything going to be okay?" I began crying, suddenly hopeful. I wanted to leave and go right back home. "I'm sorry." Sandy asked if I needed anything. I told her that I needed a suit. A suit—that's what I wanted my wife to bring me.

The woman raised her voice for the first time, letting her frustrations out with a loud, "You won't need a suit here—no suits!"

On the dining room wall in our Stanley Street house was a photo of me at Eaton's sitting on Santa's knee. I must have been three years old. I was smiling widely. Sandy and I had hung other photos along that same wall: a picture of us with the kids in Wildwood, another of the kids on the beach at Long Point. A happy, innocent, framed family. Later I would return to Stanley Street to find those photos gone, and Sandy would tell me she had smashed them all after she hung up the phone that day.

I was led by two orderlies to my room. The pills were kicking in. I dropped onto the bed and the orderlies strapped me down to the bed frame. Then I drifted into a beautiful, carefree, dreamless sleep.

It's human nature to justify one's personal condition and shortcomings by comparing them to those of someone less fortunate. So it's common, and important, when you're shovelling powder up your nose, to point out that at least you're not as bad as so-and-so. We gossiped, like old women gossip over cups of tea and pink sandwiches, only we did so over rolled-up bills and blow. "I saw this girl cut an entire gram into one line and do it in the bathroom at the Gown & Gavel," or this guy had to sell his car, or boat, or lost his house because he fell so behind on his mortgage but kept on drugging. War stories. The kind of stories I'd hear around mirrors when I was using, I would hear again in rehab. Twelve steps to heaven and all the second-hand smoke you can handle. I never bought into the "old glory" of those meetings—it was like a pissing contest for the quitters.

Family members and friends were encouraged to join in on some of the treatment sessions and lectures. Sandy showed up a few times. She tried her best to support me on the launching pad of my new clean-and-sober life, but I could see it in her face, in her eyes. She was seething on the inside but looked sympathetic and shaky on the outside.

Colin Cripps, my Junkhouse brother, was my only friend to come. He had watched me fall down the rabbit hole of minor celebrity status and all its trappings for years. He was the keeper of all the stories. Always ready for a laugh. But the joke was over. He knew it, and he was ready to stand front and centre to help me out.

I did make friends in rehab. I was sitting on a picnic table in the clinic's smoking area when Ira came driving up to the doors, stepped out of his Mercedes with a beer-can crack pipe, took one last hit and then checked himself in for a six-week addiction program. Ira and I became fast friends within the walls of the minimum security complex.

I say "minimum security" because even though there were no bars on the windows, the occupants of rehab were prisoners of circumstances we'd created in the outside world. Wives, husbands, kids, friends and employers were no longer going to support our nonsense. If we missed one of the three daily roll calls, we were tossed out with nowhere to turn. The families, the jobs, the friends were all gone, and they'd stay gone if we stepped out, or slipped up, or failed a regular drug testing. We were fucked. Stuck in minimum security.

One guy, Bernard, snuck heroin onto the floor and OD'ed an hour after being admitted. Thirty minutes after that, we all lined the hallways to watch him get wheeled away to Sunnybrook Hospital, where he would be put back together again, like Humpty Dumpty. He'd return a few days later and laugh his way through his third trip through the recovery program. Maybe this time he'd make it stick.

Kind of like me, Ira leaned towards cocaine if given a choice. But Ira was a little more pro than me. He was also a white-collar junkie. A guy who'd die with a full tank of gas, real estate and a decent financial profile. In rehab, Ira seemed like the one guy who was going to make it. He seemed smart enough and capable enough to kick the devil off his back. He also had the most to lose—the most worldly things to lose, that is. He was a money maker and a planet shaker, and if he could only resist the impulse to get cross-eyed on the base and watch the sun come up through a dirty motel window, he might just stand a chance.

I spent Christmas Eve with Ira on the empty ward of the centre. A painful night that Ira made less lonely for me. The next day, with only a skeleton crew present to watch over us, I saw my chance. I knew I could break out through the laundry room, into the parking lot and home to Hamilton. I'd have four hours, including the trip there and back, before anyone would miss me. I got the only guy I knew who'd wake up at 5 a.m. and waste his Christmas morning. That guy was Sandy's cousin, Shawn MacFarlane.

We drove back to Hamilton in the freezing blue-Christmas-morning cold. The world was still sleeping and Christmas lights stretched as far as my eye could see, from the side of the highway, across Toronto and into the darkness of the sky. The back seat of Shawn's car was full of bags of gifts that I'd hidden under my bed in my room in rehab. In an effort to save my dignity, Gary Furniss had gone out to the Yorkdale mall and picked up gifts for my kids.

I kept myself locked up dreaming the entire morning, celebrating my escape from rehab and my return home for a few precious hours. I kept feeling light until we hit the Main Street East exit ramp. Suddenly the reality of the situation melted like candle wax all over me. I was returning to the scene of the crime. Not my home. Not the home I knew and loved, at least. It wasn't going to be like that old country tear jerker "The Green, Green Grass of Home," where everyone comes running to greet the death row inmate in his dream. Instead it was just like they said it would be in rehab, that even though you might change while inside, the world outside is still suffering, hurting from all the stunts you pulled that got you here in the first place.

Shawn parked his car out on the street, but instead of going in the front door I went around the back and up the stairs that led to our living room. In the little time I had, I didn't want to wake or see Bunny and Janie. As I crept up the stairs I noticed that mine were the first footprints in the snow. No one had been out in the yard playing. The house was still. I got to the second-floor deck where on Christmases past I'd wake up early and drag a hockey stick across the snow to make the impression of the runners of Santa's sleigh and use the butt end of the stick to make reindeer hoof prints all over the deck. When the kids woke up, I'd be excited to lead them to the

evidence that Santa had come and gone while they were
sleeping.

This year there was none of that.

I stepped though the unlocked back door, Shawn following
behind me. I went straight to the corner and plugged in the
Christmas lights, then reached into my garbage bag of presents
and put the wrapped gifts under the tree. Then I went through
the kitchen and into the hallway, standing in the doorway of the
main bedroom, where Sandy and Madeline and Thompson
were sleeping together.

I walked to the end of the bed and gave out a giant "Ho Ho
Ho . . . "

The kids woke up. "Daddy!" They ran across the bed and
into my arms. "What are you doing here?" asked Madeline.
"Are you home for good now?"

"No, no, I just came by to see you guys for Christmas."
Thompson was groggy and smiling. The kids looked a bit different to me. It was all in their eyes. Not behind them but right
out front, leading their way. It was like the world had crept in
and captured a part of them. They were still joyful but I could
see they'd been hurt. Put in a place they didn't want to be. The
pain of it was what was showing, overshadowing the Christmas
they were living through.

Sandy sat up and gave a half-hearted Merry Christmas,
then put on a terry towel robe, tied up the belt and walked
around the bed past me and disappeared into the bathroom.

I took the kids to the living room. "Let's see if Santa came
by this year."

The kids were excited. Sandy on the other hand wasn't giving
up too much. She was pleasant but not loving. She put the kettle
on for tea and whispered to Shawn. I asked her if she wanted to

come watch the kids open their presents, to which she replied, "I'm coming." Two hours went by too fast. I didn't want it to end but I had to get back to rehab before they figured out I was missing.

I went out through the back door and disappeared into the frozen morning air the way I'd come.

The kids would have dinner with Sandy's family.

I'd go back and eat cafeteria turkey in my pyjamas with Ira. My first Christmas sober.

When we finally finished our time in rehab, we left behind eight weeks of living in our pyjamas and watching Leafs games and reruns of *Law & Order* and broke back into the real world. I was going home, and was about to face the fallout from my wayward-rock-star lifestyle.

I stayed off the booze and kicked coke a few years later, and never looked back. I don't know how Bernard did on the long haul. Ira went into addiction counselling for a while, but the last time I saw him he showed up unannounced and was parked out front of my house in Hamilton in another, newer top-of-the-line Lexus, taking a hit of crack from a pop can. He had twin sister hookers in the back seat and wanted me to come out and party with him. I just laughed. Laughed really hard. What else could I do? That's the last time I saw Ira.

SQUARE ONE AND HARD WOMEN

On a winter day in 1987 I came home from Kingston to tell Bunny that Sandy was pregnant. Bunny asked me what I wanted to do. Before I could tell her I wanted to be with Sandy and our baby, Bunny offered this: "We can get a hold of that baby, and raise that baby. It has been done before." When I asked her what she meant, she fell silent. Just another secret she would take to her grave.

Later, Sandy and I would drink wine into the night, lying on a shag rug. "Bunny's not your mother. You know that, right?" Sandy would ask me. And I would admit to her, and to myself, that I knew. And then in the morning I would pretend that the conversation had never happened. I had learned from Bunny how to manage lies with expert care. Hiding our secrets where no light could find them.

There were times, before I was sober, when, having run out of bounds, I would spend the night in our Crown Victoria parked in the Melrose United Church lot across the street from 82 Stanley Avenue. Sandy had made us buy that car because it had a unibody frame known to save lives in head-on collisions. She was always expecting the worst to happen, and when she could afford to take precautions, she did. I loved that car because it could accommodate my big body in times of marital strife. Those nights, I would look across at Madeline's room on the third floor. Her light would be on, and I knew she was either playing with her Barbies or flipping through a *National Geographic* or a chapter book. I pictured Thompson already asleep in bed beside Sandy. Even though I was only about thirty yards away, I would long for them and drink myself to sleep.

Those weeks spent getting sober, I realized that I would do anything to be back with my family. I wanted to be a dad. I wanted to smell my children's necks after their baths and listen to their breathing as they fell asleep. I wanted to be there when they woke up in the morning. I would find my way through any storm and manoeuvre around all obstacles to be with them.

And then one day Sandy called me in rehab. She was crying and screaming at the same time. "You have to get these women out of this house." A few days before, there had been a vicious argument. Sandy had gone down to Bunny and Janie, looking for support, hoping for love, and instead the two of them had ganged up on her. They accused her of having an affair with a professor friend who, it turned out, was a woman in a wheelchair. They blamed her for what had happened to her marriage and offered her nothing in the way of sympathy.

Sandy was no pushover, especially when she was cornered,

so she fought back and left teeth marks in their flesh. "When are you going start telling the truth around here?" she yelled.

"What do you mean?" Janie asked.

Face to face with Janie, Sandy said, "Where Tom comes from?" Words set free in the room like a bird of prey spreading its wings and coming at them to pluck out their eyes. Bunny sat silent, but Janie lunged at Sandy and yelled back, "That will go to the grave!"

I tried hard to focus on what Sandy was saying. Communication had come to a halt. Bunny and Janie had called in a locksmith. Gone was the kids' access to Bunny's breakfast table. Gone were their visits down to Grandma's. Sandy could feel the house coming apart as the seams ripped a little bit more every night, until the ceiling opened up above her bed and she could see the clouds moving across the winter sky as she lay there, silent, wide awake.

Sandy told me to get Bunny and Janie out of our house, and I picked up a pay phone in the hallway of the rehab centre and made the call. "Mom . . . things are out of hand. You and Janie are going to have to find someplace else to live."

"Okay," Bunny said. That's how simple it was. That's how easily Bunny accepted the situation. Her son was kicking her out of his house and her only response was an agreeable, "Okay."

Nothing was making any sense to me. I had just done something that would haunt me for the rest of my life, and the incident was completely without any immediate consequence. I was standing at ground zero without even a hair blown out of place. The only thing that was important to Bunny and Janie was preserving the lie, getting back to the place where everything was normal. The moment just passed, and I imagine now that they set everything back to square one without missing a beat.

In that house on Stanley Avenue, Bunny and Janie had had space enough for a new dining room set and a cabinet full of china dishes, tea cups and silverware. The two of them saved hard for this fancy setup and I remember them once calling me downstairs to show me how beautiful it all was. They dressed up in their best clothes and set the table full of dishes for what looked like an imaginary formal dinner. When I looked up from the table setting, they were smiling from ear to ear, bursting with pride. They looked so beautiful and so fragile.

I arrived home from rehab and Sandy told me I'd have to live on the first floor if I was going to stay in the house. She went upstairs and I opened the door to what had been Bunny and Janie's home. It had been emptied out, and the room where they kept their fancy dishes and dining room set was barren. They'd sold it all off to antique dealers on Locke Street for the quick cash needed to set up in an apartment over on Charlton Avenue. I sat on the floor of the deserted room and cried. We were a few weeks into the new millennium, but inside our house time hardly moved at all. It just limped through the dark hallways and staircases. Ghosts came in from the cold—memories, flashes of old parties, holiday celebrations, hopes, dreams and all that jazz that keeps us living and dying with open or broken hearts.

PLAYING SOBER

When I finally got the bottle out of my hand and the drugs out of my system, I walked around like it was my first day on earth. Sobriety was like learning to walk and talk again.

All my distractions had lost their meaning. They were still out there, still burning bright and trying to get my attention, but I was looking in the other direction. The places I used to go seemed low-definition, dim, flat and depressing. The bars I passed reminded me of Edward Hopper's *Nighthawks*. I loved that painting but there was no distant, time-travel romance in the bars around Hess Village. They all looked lonely. Holding myself together was not easy, but I kept myself on course.

The first time I was on stage after sobering up was at the Calgary Folk Festival. My manager, Allen Moy, was taking the proper precautions on my behalf. He knew I was vulnerable. He knew and I knew that I was twenty-five years into performing stoned or drunk, and the temptation was going to be turned up to ten. So he put me on a flight that landed two hours before I was due on stage, then had a limo drive me directly behind the stage, where I had little chance of wandering off into a minefield of fans and fast friends. The limo waited behind the stage until the show was over, I walked off, got back in, was taken directly to the airport and flown home.

I remember we were playing as a trio, just Stephen, Colin and me. No drums, no bass. It was a hot late afternoon, and the lawn in front of the stage was looking about seven thousand strong. I felt good—no nerves, no butterflies. I sat in the dressing room tuning up, then I put on my suit and walked out on stage with Colin and Stephen.

We hit the top of Fred Eaglesmith's "49 Tons" like a plane taking off. Completely united. Then we played "Lean on Your Peers," "Red Dress" and "Patience of a Working Man." It felt great. I felt great.

Light and easy and in the groove. In fact, I felt better than I could ever remember feeling playing music. I couldn't put my finger on why, but like a flash, it hit me: I was sober. I was on stage sober for the first time in my life, and I was in heaven. I sang in pitch and my rhythm was better than ever. I never wanted to play music any other way.

This was it. I had arrived. I was so attached to the music, every note. *Life is going to be so much easier now*, I thought on the way back to the airport. We survive, and with those skills, and in that survival, we create art.

DEATH OF A WARRIOR—TWO

I put the spirit of Bunny into everything I did. She was everywhere. She was in my art, my day-to-day life. Her brutal and inappropriate observations and her irreverent, rebel attitude stood beside me, guiding me through a world of bullshit. But most especially she was in my relationships. Growing up on East 36th Street I became aware of Diana Belfor, a young woman who was dating two or three boys at the same time. Bunny was aware of her too. She would watch Diana Belfor walk home with different dates each night, and she remarked to me at the timely age of seven or eight that Diana's "legs were pleasure bent from opening them too much for the neighbourhood boys." This has an effect on a young boy. Bunny always said if I decided to get married, I should keep a couple of women on the side. Advice I took to heart that turned out not to serve me well.

Sandy and I had a connection and we never really stopped loving each other, like we loved our kids, but in all the wreckage we couldn't put our relationship back together. When we split up for good in 2002, I missed the warmth of the family life we had once had together. I was separated from it, as if it was trapped inside a snow globe. But through our children we stayed intimately connected. We formed a secret society—Madeline, Thompson, Sandy and me—and somehow there happened always to be a dog in the room with us too. We worked yearly, monthly, weekly to keep the club together.

It was July 8, 2010. I was heading over to Sandy's house for Thompson's birthday party. I'd voiced a commercial in Toronto for Pontiac that afternoon. I had bought Thompson a bike and had arranged for it to be ready for pickup when I got off the GO bus from Toronto on Main Street West by McMaster. I walked over to the bike shop in Westdale and rode the bike across town. Instead of taking on the busy streets and the hazardous off-ramps from the 403, I decided to glide down the hill at Longwood and tool along the Desjardins Recreational Trail, a wooden walkway that joined stylish Westdale with the old-world, blue-collar North End.

I called the trail "the porthole" because the first time I walked it back in the nineties, I noticed that somewhere in the middle, two levels of society, rarely seen together, met. Coming from the west you'd see white-bread, neon-coloured, Lycra-clad, headphoned, pinched-nosed joggers and cyclists speeding head-on into black-clad Italian and Portuguese widows, biker chicks being dragged along by pit bulls and guys riding old ten-speeds with cases of beer on the handlebars.

As I arrived at Sandy's, I received a call from Janie. She was at St. Olga's retirement home. Bunny was dying, I should come quickly if I wanted to see her before she went. I paid heed; this, at least, was not a mistake I would make twice.

Bunny Wilson gave everything she had to us. Janie, Thompson, Madeline, me and especially George. Bunny was a warrior, and now she was dying. The feeling I had first had when I was four years old came back again. The fear of Bunny's death, the fear I could not live without her. Thompson and Madeline immediately stood up and walked out of the party. We headed over to St. Olga's. I sat at Bunny's bedside. The room thick with the smell of old—not death, just old. The late afternoon sun travelling over King Street West, beating through the windows and off the walls in Bunny's room. Firing straight into the corner and onto the single bed where Bunny lay, still and silent, the light surrounding her frail, blanketed body. I thought of the Bible-story painting on the wall of St. John United Church on East 38th Street. And I thought that I could roll away her stone, just like Jesus, and Bunny would stand up, and I would take her to Swiss Chalet for a quarter chicken dinner and we would have a couple of laughs.

But Bunny remained silent and still, the way she had been for months. It was hard to tell what, if anything, had changed. It was hard to tell that now she was finally dying. Bunny had suffered from Alzheimer's for seven years, and the disease had moved in and made itself comfortable before anyone even noticed. But then Bunny's eyes glazed over, her face changed, she stopped recognizing herself in the mirror. Like it had with George years before, time faded away until Bunny's simple functions shut down. She could not swallow solid food. And then finally she could not swallow fluids.

I sat in the chair beside her bed for hours. I don't remember speaking. Not to Janie. Not to Thompson or Madeline, not to the nurses. Not to Sandy, who arrived later. Even Madeline's dog Phil, a rescued coon hound who was out of control almost all the time, was flat out on the floor, awake but in a state of quiet reflection. The sun went down without me noticing. The lights came on above Bunny's bed, and I just stared at her short white hair on the pillow.

For the next day and a half, it seemed, none of us left. We didn't have to. We were already home. We sat with Bunny and waited for mercy to take her away.

Rain is my summertime salvation. When the house gets dull and dark and still, and the few cars that pass swish small ocean swells over the sidewalks and onto the grass, I feel safe.

My annual fight with summertime depression is no big deal really. It happens every day between 4 and 9 p.m. from late May to mid-September. Let's just call it four months, or 122 days, or better still, 610 solid, relentless hours every year since I was about five years old. I've been fighting this feeling ever since Bunny and George used to shut the house down after the daily five o'clock suppertime hour and ready themselves for a long summer sleep.

I talk about Bunny in all sorts of ways, and I toss her flaws and cracks into the mix of memories of her. But late at night, when the noise gets turned down, it's different. I lie awake thinking about Bunny and her massive, loving heart.

Every day I wish she was here.

I want to hear her voice and touch the thin skin on her hands and face. I want to laugh at her wisecracks and hear about her pain and know how she commanded her secrets to lie low. To stay in the dark corners. She was like a spy. Living undercover. Protecting me from who I was.

If Bunny Wilson were here, I'd ask her to tell me all the things she remembers about me growing up. How she saw me. How she didn't see me. I want to add it up and subtract it. I want her side of the story. The way she saw me fitting in. How she tried to make it work. How exhausting it must have been to have a baby, live with a child and watch a wild spirit and a beast come of age. She accepted me regardless of how far out I went. Drugs, women, disappearing acts, music and desires and addictions she could not confine. She watched me make incredible mistakes. Watched me drive my life into the ditch. I hope she knows I finally crawled back out to be a better man. The man she intended me to be. The man she hoped she'd raised.

TRUTH

THE TRUTH

The truth is a constant seeker, a warrior with the tenacity of a travelling salesman, knocking on every door, looking to make its heavy-hearted delivery to exactly the right person.

When I was small, the truth was whispered by my ancestors, who sat under the dull glare of out-of-fashion Bakelite lamps while I peered out between the bars of my cheap wooden playpen. The truth disguised itself to me. Sometimes it was an alien landing saucers in my backyard outside my bedroom window. Once, after I got my tonsils out, the truth appeared to me in chloroform hallucinations. Druggy, dreamy, lost information that bobbed and weaved and staggered its way to my bedside like a drunken father home from the Legion.

For years after, the truth strangled me with its unknown details and made me question myself and attempt to shut out love and drove me to countless attempts at self-destruction. The truth left me paralyzed and gasping for breath, struggling to free my voice from deep inside my guts in the middle of the night while I was sleeping.

I trick myself into believing that I hunted down the truth. But the truth found me, and it wasn't the harmless, lily-white right-thing-to-do that we're taught it is in grade school, and there were no immediate rewards from it. The truth is a fucker.

I was fifty-three, a slightly overweight grandfather of two, a bad cook and a recovering alcoholic and drug addict. I'd been hired to join some publishers, music supervisors and SOCAN members to do some speaking gigs on the creative process and songwriting. For an hour at a time I'd talk to green writers and artists about surviving in a world that does not need what they have to offer. It was an easy hour to kill. My entire life I'd been struggling to maintain my self-respect while doing whatever it was that I wanted to do creatively, dodging depression and criticism and resisting the urge to find a closet to hang myself in. It was work I liked. I could be honest and still try to motivate my audience. It's work that took me to colleges and universities, medical conferences and corporations. I'd start my lecture with a simple line. "If you don't have to do this, don't. If you don't have the burning desire to wake up and create something, if your life does not depend on it, then please stop. You'll end up wasting your time and time of anyone who crosses paths with your creation." I would look back into the eyes of my audience and I see them thinking, "I can't believe I spent all this money to get lectured to by a guy who looks like he sleeps in his car."

I packed up a small bag and the guitar and put them by my front door and made myself some lunch and hung around the house waiting for the limo to take me to the airport. The knock came. The PR company's handler and coordinator was a young woman—when I say "young" I mean she must have been about thirty-four or thirty-five, so not that young really but young to me. I knew she was Mary Simon, a singer and songwriter from around town, but I couldn't remember if I had met her before. I have a terrible memory for names and faces and as a result I am constantly offending people by not knowing who they are. People can be very sensitive about this kind of thing, I've learned. Mary stood in my doorway putting her hands out to take my bag and my guitar. "You might have to pay me and get me where I've gotta be and tuck me in and wake me up in the morning, but you don't have to carry my luggage or put up with any of my shit, okay?" I told her.

I walked down my stone pathway through my garden, past the fountain on my lawn and up the stairs to the sidewalk, dropped my guitar and my bag into the hands of the limousine driver, walked around, opened the back door and jumped into the back seat of the limo.

It was within a minute of the car rolling down the street and turning onto Kent Street that Mary proclaimed that this was going to be a great three-day trip. "We're going to Regina and Winnipeg, and I'm really happy that you're coming out because I'm a fan of your work and you don't know this but I've been wanting to talk to you for a long time because my family and your family were friends years ago here in Hamilton and . . ."

I stopped her there. I looked at her, told her no offence but I'd heard that family-friends stuff before, mainly because of my last name. Wilson is common everywhere but seems to be especially so in Hamilton. I told Mary that my mom and dad didn't have any friends here in Hamilton. They barely talked to any of the neighbours. They were older, like in their late fifties–early sixties when I was a kid, and my father, who was a tail gunner in a Lancaster bomber, was blinded in the Second World War. His massive head injury made him shut down and uninterested in people's company as a result of years in the torching dark. He wasn't comfortable making friends. So even though Mary thought her family was friends with my family, I could tell her that they probably weren't. The only people that were even allowed in our house were some relatives who came down from Quebec: a collection of ragged aunts, cousins and one Mohawk uncle that was actually my aunt's boyfriend, and they were all from my mother's side of the family.

"Oh no, no, no," she said. "My grandmother Mary Brennan. She was best friends with your mother, Bunny."

"Mary Brennan? Your grandmother was Mary Brennan? I remember your grandmother. I remember her name but I haven't heard it in about fifty years. I was just little when she used to come around and I forgot about her completely until now."

I felt myself soften, realizing after all these years that Bunny actually had a friend here in Hamilton. I thought that she was a complete loner, sometimes bordering on lonely, sitting at the table with only blind George to keep her company, drinking rum, smoking cigarettes, playing cards. "So no shit, eh? Mary Brennan."

"Yeah, they were really close. Best friends for a while, I heard. In fact, they were so close that my grandmother was there when Bunny and George adopted you . . ."

"What?

"Wait . . . What?

"I don't know what you're talking about . . ."

She looked at me, shocked. Her mouth actually fell open. "Shut up. . . . Fuck off. . . . Don't kid around, Tom, don't fuck with me like you never knew you were adopted."

I don't remember anything for a while after that. The limo was speeding down the QEW heading to the airport, and I must have fallen into a dream. My mind flew past the traffic and straight up over the hydro towers and the rooftops and I was gone.

DRIVING JANIE HOME

I have a video of Thompson's third birthday party. In it Janie and Bunny stand shoulder to shoulder, just outside the madness that encircles the birthday boy: kids yelling; Sandy marching the cake, all lit up, through the room; Madeline trying hard to be in the centre of the action, spinning on one foot and sucking up all the energy like it was ginger ale; Thompson happy and calm as ever; and Ralph Nicole and me stoned, playing guitars and singing "She'll Be Coming 'Round the Mountain," "Old MacDonald Had a Farm," "This Old Man," and "Bud the Spud." And then about five feet back from it all, Janie and Bunny, dressed like they're going to church, stylish, ironed and arranged, ready for high tea or a meeting with the priest.

Bunny was quietly in charge, letting Sandy and me be parents, but I can tell by her face in the video that she was just barely keeping her cool. Janie was beside her; together they formed the two-headed matriarch of our family. After Bunny died, Janie assumed matriarchal duties on her own. Janie went to the head of the table for Thanksgiving, Christmas and family birthdays. And it was on the occasion of another birthday, my own, that I finally drummed up the courage to ask her questions that had been burning inside me since Mary Simon had revealed the secret of my adoption three years before.

Of course, questions had been swirling around Janie long before that fateful drive to the airport. Women in my life were all too comfortable voicing their suspicions. For example, when I first started seeing Cathy Jones a decade or so before. Cathy was a five-sided coin, a Newfoundlander with a beautiful heart and a knee-jerk honesty that could hurt if you were in her line of fire. We met and fell in love on the spot. She and her boyfriend came to a Blackie and the Rodeo Kings show at Barrymore's in Ottawa. We got right into it fast—instant friends—flirting and laughing until her boyfriend came up to us and asked how things were going. Cathy turned and gave him her report plain and simple: "I'm going home with him" and pointed across the table at me. So perhaps not surprisingly she took one look at Janie, one look at Bunny, then back at me and bellowed out, "There is no fuckin' way Bunny is your mother. She's too old, Tom. Janie has to be your mother. And I'm going to find out for myself if you don't." More than once I'd have to pull Cathy back into her seat and tell her no. We had a four-year love affair that was so intense we should have known it wasn't going to last, and it didn't.

Later, a different girlfriend, Andrea Ramalo, was beyond persistent. I think she was attracted to the possibility of my Mohawk blood raising exotic interest on the white-bread Queen Street art scene. It seemed like she woke up every morning asking me when I was going to talk to Janie, and asked the same question as I closed my eyes to go to sleep at night.

Mostly I was annoyed by how confident these women were in their opinions, how willing they were to instruct me on how to deal with my family, my life. Ultimately I'm kind of thankful to them for edging me closer to the truth. But what they didn't understand was that it was my story, my life, and I'd deal with it when I was good and ready to deal with it. Not a second sooner.

Now that second had arrived.

It was my fifty-sixth birthday party, and I was about to drive Janie home. She always likes to leave the party early; she likes to waltz through the door as dinner is hitting the table and gets the hell out when the dishes are being cleared. I walked her out to an old van that Thompson used for his band Harlan Pepper and buckled her into the passenger seat. We drove off down Amelia and Kent streets, then across Aberdeen to Bay and around a few more corners to her apartment on Charlton Avenue.

I pulled into the driveway and through to the back parking lot of her apartment building. The June sun beat down on the windshield and I began to sweat. I tried to stay calm, but my thoughts were racing around in my head and I became more animated. My voice got louder and more direct, and my hands flew in front of me as I spoke.

There were questions I wanted to ask, but I needed to make sure Janie had a way out, that she'd be able to open the van door and disappear into her apartment without much effort. I wanted to make it easy on Janie. So I slowed my mind down and grabbed the steering wheel to keep my hands still. I started out nice and

cool, like I was pointing out a blue jay or a robin dropping down
on the lawn in front of us.

"Hey, Janie. I found out a couple of years ago that Mom
and Dad weren't my real mom and dad. They weren't my birth
parents, anyway, and you're the only relative I have now. You
were also really close to Bunny, so if at any time in the future
you remember anything about where I came from, anything
you'd feel comfortable sharing with me, please do."

She asked me how I found out. I said that Mary Brennan's
granddaughter had told me.

"That damn Mary Brennan. She always had a big mouth,"
Janie said.

"Well . . . okay, yeah," I said.

What happened next, happened fast, and was so final it left
me numb. Words that had been tied down to railroad tracks for
fifty-six years broke free and shot across the fields—liberated
truth in such full colour it made me dizzy.

Janie turned to me and her eyes teared up. "I'm sorry, Tom.
I don't know how to say this. I hope you forgive me . . . I'm your
mother."

I stared straight ahead at the wall of Janie's apartment
building for what seemed an eternity. You know how they say
your life flashes before your eyes when you're about to die? Well
the same happens when you're being reborn.

Janie began to cry, and I put my arms around her and told
her it was okay. Now I could finally be there to take care of her,
to protect her. I wanted her to know that the secret she'd been
keeping was not going to change how much I loved her.

The truth was out, and this moment was ours and no one
else's. I leaned back in my seat and followed my instincts. Here
we were, mother and son for only the second time in our lives,

and my first act was to keep her on the sunny side of the street.

"It's okay, Janie. Don't worry about a thing. Everything is going to be just like it's always been. Better in fact. Nothing is going to go wrong. I'll make certain of that. You're still Janie to the kids. You're still Janie to the grandsons and all our friends and family."

It was hard to believe that it was this easy. From the back of my mind it seemed impossible; from deep in my heart it was simply forbidden. But in reality it all came down to Janie and me, and nothing could hold us down this time. In the end, all it took was one drive home together.

A MOTHER CONFESSES

Janie is my mother. I still call her Janie, and so do her grand-children, Madeline and Thompson, and so do Madeline's boys, Janie's two great-grandsons. Janie and I both come from places where our options were limited. Janie comes from Kahnawake. I come from Janie. We circled around one another for fifty-six years, never coming clean and never acknowledging the obvious. For two people to manage this situation is a full-time job. You've got to look the other way at exactly the right moment or the other person will catch you being yourself. Being the son, being the mother. The effort took its toll on us both.

Janie lived with Bunny and George after they took me in on East 36th Street, but by all reports she wasn't allowed to bathe me or feed me or put me down to sleep or comfort me when I cried. I can't begin to imagine the mental torture she went through being that close to her own baby and not being able to care for him. Him—me. That was me.

Despite her generous and loving heart, Bunny made her secret, this lie, her full-time job until the day she died. "There are secrets I know about you that I'll take to my grave," and by Jesus she did. I knew I was an outsider. I knew I was in the wrong place. I knew I was supposed to be somewhere else, but I didn't know where that place was, or even how to find it on a map.

I wonder what kind of life we all would have had if we'd known who we were. What kind of people we would have been if the lock and key were tossed away, if our roles were defined and our hearts were free. If we had been allowed to make the mistakes, to love and be loved on our own terms.

Janie has a busy life. She has a job counting communion dollars at her church. She and her sister Millie join seniors groups and friends and go on day trips to Niagara-on-the-Lake, St. George and in and around Hamilton. She has doctor and hair appointments. She and Millie share an apartment, and Janie takes on a lot of the domestic duties. Once Janie makes plans, that's that—she sticks to them like they're the word of the Lord Jesus himself. She'll respectfully blow off a family gathering if she has something on the go. This can sometimes lead to hurt feelings, including my own, but I admire her determination and I'm happy she keeps busy, keeps moving. That's how she's been all her life; it's how she survives.

I drive Janie around town to help her with her errands and it's on these occasions that we get to catch up. When I say "catch up," I mean fill in the massive gaps of information missing from our story: my story, and her story before me. Once in my car,

Janie is mild-mannered and polite as always. She proceeds cautiously. As though reading from a script, she speaks about growing up on the reserve, about her mom and dad and her journey to Toronto, about Bunny and George and the day I was born. I usually don't have to ask the first question and I never challenge the details. I just accept what she says because I know life has been hard on her and that reliving it—saying it out loud—is harder still.

My minivan is her confessional and I'm her priest. Janie trusts me and knows I'm interested in her story. All of it. Every detail is like a colour filling in a blank space on our canvas. Janie wants me in on "our" history. Maybe she's been waiting a lifetime to explain how our lives came to be sealed up tight in different envelopes.

We have a limited amount of time between the front door of her apartment and Fortinos grocery store, Lime Ridge Mall or Ikea, but I keep my ears open and try to remember the details and the characters she tells me about. My story comes from Janie's side of the street only, and that's good enough for me. She has opinions. She has facts. She has the key to so many doors, and often she has tears to accompany her words.

The River-View in Chateauguay was the Mohawk hang. The air in the place was filled with smoke and sweat, fists, laughter and lies, and Ernest Tubb and Buddy Holly on the jukebox and the booze going down hard. Reserve buddies with their New York State plates gathered there nightly. They swaggered and strutted and flirted like great brown-skinned giants. Skywalkers and lacrosse stars and Mohawk con men, gangsters, warriors— players all of them, showing off some Mohawk handsome. Just how handsome can a human being be? Mohawk handsome, that's how.

Women swooned across the dance floor and out the back door of the bar, their skirts magically flying over their heads, their panties dropping and their bras coming undone in a swirl of high-heeled drunken passion. I can't imagine how many kids were conceived in the back seats of the cars that tore out of the River-View parking lot at closing time, out onto dirt roads that ended in some field wet with dew from the damp summer night, and lit by blue rays of the holier than holy Quebec moonlight.

Eighteen-year-old Janie took what she had down the road to Chateauguay one night with the hope that she could just keep on going. She went to the River-View to try to kill her demons, to figure herself out and get away from her home and family and feel a part of the world. Thirty-something Rudy West was at the River-View the night Janie and her friend stepped through the front door and into the thick barroom air. He beelined over to Janie and said the things she wanted to hear. She knocked back his free drinks and sucked back his words and smiled and spun around the dance floor.

They ended up running off to get married.

"How long had you known him before you ran off to New York? A few weeks or so?" I asked.

"Oh, no, no. It was more like a few hours. We left right from the River-View that night."

"What?" I couldn't stop laughing. I always thought I was the wild-hearted rounder in the family.

Janie had nothing to lose. She was ready to take whatever chances she needed to take to get out. They drove straight through the reserve and disappeared in the shadows between the trees. They skidded along the backroads through Saint-Rémi,

Saint-Michel, Saint-Édouard, Sherrington, over the border and down into Champlain, Vermont, and out into the unprotected wilds of America. She'd never been over the border. She'd never been this far from home on her own. They had a clear path straight down the spine of the state towards New York City, where West worked up in the sky during the week.

They wound through the streets, and he took them down to the south end of the island to stay in a hotel on the Bowery. He was playing the little big man, full of bluster and promises. He talked of getting married and of setting Janie up in an apartment.

They left Manhattan and headed over the East River to State Street into the heart of Little Caughnawaga. The ten square blocks housed the working men and the families that migrated down from Kahnawake to build the iconic New York skyline, its bridges, its monuments to modernity.

So many familiar faces, some Janie had not seen in years, the faces of her neighbours and family in Quebec. But those who had been in Brooklyn for a while, some who had been born there, spoke in a Flatbush accent. Mohawk was the native tongue in that little ten-block area. It was spoken in the bars and on the job sites, but a lot of parents spoke only English to their kids, a trickle-down effect of residential schools, where the language of their ancestors had been punched out of them.

They poured out of three-storey walk-ups and into the streets, flooding the sidewalks, the grocery stores and the famous Mohawk watering hole the Pow Wow. West took Janie there to show her off. He was reckless and the locals took notice. Word was spreading about the Lazare girl, the daughter of Chief John Lazare himself, who had suddenly disappeared from the River-View. The same eyes and ears that spread word and kept secrets back home in Quebec were kept open on one another in Brooklyn.

Janie was getting restless. She'd escaped the reserve and was in one of the world's great cities, but she was stuck with ol' Rudy West poking at her, crowding her and showing her off. She must have felt sick about her misjudgment, but she was saved somewhere into the second week of her time in Brooklyn. From back in Kahnawake, West's mother called him up and told him firm, fast and straight that word had spread, the family was looking for their daughter and he'd better send Janie back right now.

Janie watched West's coolness melt away as she listened to his mother reprimanding him over the phone. John Lazare was angry and was going to send people out to find her, drag her home and maybe leave him floating in the East River. He hung up the phone, turned to Janie and said, "You gotta go home." And then he said, "Anyway, I'm a married man."

Janie said, "What? You're a married man? You didn't tell me that, you told me you were free."

He said, "I had plans, I really did. I planned for you and me to get something going down here."

What he wanted was the classic routine of keeping two wives, two families in two households in two cities. Not much of a plan, but a fairly common situation for truckers and steelworkers and long-term migrants working away from the homestead.

Janie said, "Well, I'm going home right now." He got her ticket and he brought her to the bus depot on 42nd Street in Manhattan. She'd had a taste of what a young girl craves— bright lights, big city—but how humiliated and defeated she must have been. She showed her face among the ironworkers and their families in Brooklyn, and the word burned up the telephone wires, sizzled north and all the way back home.

Sitting at the back of a Greyhound bus edging up the west

side of Manhattan and along the Hudson, she watched the city bounce off her window and into eternity. She looked out at New York City for the last time, for the last time in her life, devastated as she prepared for the hard fist of judgment to come down on her when she skulked back to Quebec, a foolish teenager who'd bought into the empty promises of a married man, a pregnant eighteen-year-old as desperate as she could be.

MOHAWK LEGENDS

You can't fool kids. Especially not the mouthy fists-first, piss-and-spit Hamilton kids who told me straight out that I looked like an Indian. I was called a wahoo, a chief and a savage. Later the insults became uglier: "You big ugly fuckin' Indian." In gym class, kids put two fingers behind their heads as feathers, and they slapped their hands against their mouths going "Awe-wa-wa-wa . . . Awe-wa-wa-wa-wa," dancing around me in old cartoon style. I asked Bunny if I had Indian blood. She told me to stop being so foolish. "How could you ask such a question in front of your father who fought in the war and got blinded, just to come home and face a question like this?"

Turns out you really can't fool kids. I am a Mohawk. The son of a skywalker. From Janie's story, I knew just enough about

Rudy West to research him online. I discovered that he was already dead. Good, I thought, fuck him. I would never know him, but I did know John Lazare, and through him was connected to the legends of my Mohawk ancestors.

I used to spend some Christmases at John Lazare's house. He was Uncle John to me then. He'd pull money from behind my ears like a grandfather would. He told me his stories. He was an immaculately dressed man and always kept his shoes polished and neatly lined up on the staircase in his home. One morning, Janie noticed that all his left shoes were missing from the staircase order. They were gathered in a pile at the bottom of the stairs, as if a hand from the underworld had taken them all out. Later that same day a pickup rammed into the oil-delivery truck John was unloading. As a result of the accident, his left leg was amputated. Whenever I saw him he'd get me to punch his wooden leg so my knuckles hurt.

He told me that, one night, walking across the Mercier Bridge after work in Lasalle, he noticed a ball of fire dancing on the water below him. He thought he was seeing things. He got closer until he was standing on the bridge directly above the fireball. He was certain what he saw was real. So certain that he went straight home and told his father.

His father, Peter Lazare, explained it was a premonition. The fire of a burning soul. The soul of someone who was not dead yet. He told his son to return to the river the next night to see if the ball of fire would reappear.

John went back to the river and stood under the Mercier Bridge. He saw a barge and police and a crane pulling a car out of the river. He looked up to where he had been standing the night before and saw the guard rail was broken. A car had sped through it and down into the cold Saint Lawrence River.

I remember John Lazare told this story with unbreakable concentration; it had obviously affected him deeply. Even then I was honoured that he would share it with me. Now I know it was my grandfather who told me the story as part of a Mohawk tradition of passing on the legends of our ancestors and our community.

When I was growing up, John's brother Sonny Lazare was a living legend to me. He was an ironworker, one of the wild daredevils who rolled with the clouds and swung from the stars. People thought the skywalkers were fearless, but they were just as afraid of falling as the next guy. They just didn't talk about it. Under the Quebec bridge on the eastern side there's a steel cross erected in memory of the men who fell to their deaths when the bridge collapsed in 1907. Thirty-three men from Kahnawake died working on that bridge. After that, the women got together and told the men they didn't want such a large group of Mohawk men working together on one job ever again. But time passed, and the men did what they felt they needed to do.

Every Sunday the men ate their dinner at six and were in bed at seven p.m. At midnight they were up again, and while their families slept, they'd stumble into cars with four other guys and hit the road. The weekly drives back to New York were like high-speed funeral processions, with the passengers sitting mouths agape, heads bowed into chests, while the driver made the five-hour journey. They were sleeping cars, and when everyone woke up, they were in Brooklyn, just in time for work.

Sonny Lazare was an ironworker in Detroit. His name was often mentioned in Bunny's kitchen during long-distance phone calls or in conversations at the table with Janie. In fact, news from "back home" was at the centre of most conversations when I was a kid. I'd sit under the kitchen table playing with

Dinky and Matchbox cars while the tales rolled out. I heard the many theories discussed about the murder of wrestler Don Eagle, an American Wrestling Association champ. The news reported a single self-inflicted gunshot wound to his head. My kitchen experts thought the mob had killed Don Eagle, or that his wife, Jean, had. It was said that she had suffered one beating too many at the hands of Eagle. She mysteriously disappeared to Florida, where she was murdered and burned in a torched car and later found by a chief of Kahnawake.

I was quiet while they spoke, chilled by the details of the torched car, burned body and wrestling star. I imagined it as an episode of *The Twilight Zone*, the headlines bold in black and white. The mystic reserve and its secrets captured my imagination by the time I was five or six years old. The world Janie and Bunny talked about was thousands of dark nights away from mine on East 36th Street, but the stories got inside me. I swear I walked those dirt roads in my dreams, in visions just before the voices in the kitchen faded to black and my mind dropped into the sleep hole. Down into a world of shape-shifters, dogs and men chasing me, and hoofed women calling out to me, where I was led by my ancestors through the trees. I was safe in those visions, protected and guided from danger by a great bear that I felt behind me at all times. I stood there looking up at car crashes on the Mercier Bridge, the midnight trains blowing their tops and rattling the town's windows as they passed. I rode to safety on the backs of giant turtles that turned into relatives, and ghosts that showed themselves to remind me where I was going and where I was from, and the Saint Lawrence Seaway screamed as it rushed past.

ON THE DAY I WAS BORN

It was embarrassing for the family. John Lazare was a strict man and it was shameful to have a daughter who was that young, unmarried and pregnant. They were all Catholics, after all. Janie had to be kept out of sight. She was forced to stay across the highway, off the reserve, until John could figure out what to do with her. She was eventually told she'd have to leave. They shipped her out under the cover of night to Bunny and George Wilson's in Hamilton. Back to the people who took her in during times of sickness. She got on a train and said good-bye to her home and family again and headed west to Southern Ontario.

On the morning I was born, the hot sun bloomed along the Niagara Escarpment and the first colours of the day rolled down the Jolley Cut, filling the streets of Hamilton like a blood-soaked towel. I left the pain and sadness of my mother's body and entered the June day in the coolness of the Catholic hospital. Saint Joseph had received me, and my mother was alone, broken-hearted, and not sure what was going to happen next. The hardest part was over. The hardest part had just begun.

She was told that she couldn't be a mother, that she didn't know how. She was riding on the rim of a mental breakdown. She was sedated and kept behind hospital doors for observation, and by the time she got out I was in a Catholic-services orphan nursery where I would start my life cared for by nuns among the other unwanted babies. The babies of drunken, careless lovers, mental patients, rape victims and underage girls who were looking for a lucky break or a second chance.

A few months later the Millers, who had two children of their own, scooped me up to bring me into their home near Fennell Square. My life was set. I am told the Millers loved me. They wanted to adopt me, make me a Miller.

None of this was going down well back home in Kahnawake. John Lazare and his brother Sonny didn't like the idea of one of theirs being raised outside the family, off the reserve, by people they didn't know. Sonny, already the father of seven children, suggested he and his wife, Hazel, would take me in.

John rolled into town in his Buick Riviera. He drove straight to Bunny and George's midtown apartment where Janie was living. He announced that he was here to take his grandson back and demanded to know where I was.

Janie told her father I'd been chosen by a very nice family and that she had been to visit me and they were going to adopt me as soon as they were allowed. "Get those people on the

phone and tell them we're on our way. Make the arrangements,"
John said to Bunny.

Bunny made the call, and John and Janie got in his car and
headed up the Jolley Cut to Concession Street and landed at the
front door of the Millers. Janie said she'd changed her mind
and no longer wanted to give her baby to them. So I was taken
from the only family I'd known and brought back to Bunny and
George's apartment on Barnesdale Boulevard. And then Bunny
Wilson made a decision. She did not want the baby taken up to
the reserve, where Janie had been treated so badly. A doctor had
told Bunny that Janie's emotional state was so fragile that if she
was any more broken-hearted she would die. Bunny told Janie
and John that she and George would adopt me and Janie could
stay with them too. The baby would be kept in the family, not
raised by strangers, and so John agreed to the plan.

Soon after, Bunny and George moved to the house on
36th Street with their young niece and their baby son Thomas
Cunningham Wilson.

"I tracked down the doctor who delivered me," I tell Janie in
the quiet of our confessional. "I asked him for my adoption
papers and he told me there are none. I was never legally
adopted. I was just signed over to Bunny and George, and the
names on my birth certificate were changed from yours and
Rudy West's to Beatrice and George Wilson's."

"That's too bad," Janie tells me. "Bunny told me she had
adopted you."

"And what about my name? Who named me Tommy?"

"When you were born, I wanted to call you Thomas
George, but Bunny thought it was too Native. I said that was
important, but Bunny said no. So you were called Thomas
Cunningham after George Wilson's father. To tell you the

truth, Bunny wanted to hide that you were an Indian. She wanted everyone to think she had you. She hid the truth from everyone, and anyone who suspected or knew any different was banished. Look at her best friend, Bea LaSalle from Sun Life. She used to come and visit all the time. She must have said something about you being adopted. Bunny cut her out and never saw her again."

On this one occasion I allow myself a bit of frustration, maybe even anger. "So George is gone, Bunny is gone, and here I am fifty-six years old. It's all out in the open. It's exhausting to think of all that effort for nothing. Isn't the truth an easier route to take?"

"I don't know. I tried to be good to Bunny, and she was good to me. She adopted you but she didn't want you to know. That was the deal. She would take you if I agreed to seal my lips. But I always suspected you knew. I said to her, I said Tom knows and I think he's going to put two and two together."

WAKING UP—TWO

My name is Thomas George Lazare.

I come from a family of Mohawk chiefs. Peacemakers and peacekeepers, fighters and man-eaters. Lacrosse magicians, tobacco salesmen, gangsters, shamans, shit disturbers and survivors. But instead of growing up around these heroes and zeros, I grew up on the East Mountain in Hamilton, Ontario, the son of a blind war vet and a French-Canadian she-warrior.

I am a living breathing lie. An embarrassment. A married man's mistake and a young girl's only chance to hop a fence out of town and escape to freedom. I was hidden from the world and from myself, my name was changed because it sounded too Indian and my clothes were fitted to look like the other kids'.

191

I've been Thomas Cunningham Wilson ever since. An Irish-French kid. Not Indian—no way. No Indian blood in me. None. Zero.

I knew the truth but I swallowed up the lies. I second-guessed myself. I felt guilty for doubting what I was told. I dreamed myself into fields where I thought I belonged. I got onboard space ships and woke up in cold sweats not knowing who I was or where I came from. I took many stabs at it as a kid, trying to figure it out, lying in bed thinking it over and feeling like I had fallen down a rabbit hole. I was a kid dressed like a prop, all short pants and bow ties. Dressed like I was going to a picnic with Winnie the Pooh, like a post-war upper-class twit.

I think Bunny modelled me after Prince Charles. Hell, she didn't know how to dress a kid. She had no feel for it. All she wanted to do was make me less Indian than I was. And some short pants with high socks and a white shirt with a blazer might draw attention away from my Mohawk features and the fact that I had a giant head that looked like it was carved from a spruce tree. And then as I got older, I was just bigger than Bunny and George. Like a giant compared to them. Like Will Ferrell to Bob Newhart in the movie *Elf*.

I was sent out into the world as a kid who was from "over there" somewhere, a European kid when it was evident from looking at me that I was from here. I was from deep in the earth I stood upon. A Native North American among a people from another planet.

SISTERS

After Bunny and George became my parents, Janie got a job working for a periodontist downtown. She caught the Upper Sherman at the stop over on Brucedale Avenue. She ran into Mrs. Miller regularly but never spoke to her. She never raised her head when Mrs. Miller got on the bus. Just sat there silent, staring down at a gum wrapper or a cigarette butt on the bus floor.

All day she thought about me. All day she thought of ways to distract Bunny so she could get her hands on me. Hold me. All day her arms ached for me. She thought she was going crazy. Her desire for her baby was consuming her. But every day she got home from work, she watched me from a safe distance. Watched Bunny feed me Gerber baby food from a jar and burp me while George sat at the kitchen table.

One night George got really drunk. He grabbed his cane and swung it around the kitchen, knocking all of Bunny's dishes off the shelves. He started yelling at Janie. He pushed her against the wall and told her to get the hell out. "You see the door? Take it—get out of here."

Janie didn't understand. She was following the rules, minding her business, staying quiet, keeping away from the baby, but something went wrong. She kneeled down in a corner of the kitchen. She covered her ears with her hands and closed her eyes, cried and wished she could disappear from there. But instead she stood up to face George. She told him, "If that's what you want, George, I understand. Don't worry, I will be out of this house by the end of the week."

Bunny said nothing. Not a word.

Janie marched out of the house the next morning and knocked on a door of a house advertising a room for rent, on James Street just a few blocks south from her work. She walked in and rented a bed and a sitting room with a shared kitchen and bathroom. She gave a deposit, and after work that day went back to Bunny and George's and packed up her things. Still Bunny said nothing. Not a word.

Janie stayed downtown, off the East Mountain and away from 162 East 36th Street altogether. She kept to herself, worked, read books, went to movies alone and every so often took the bus into Toronto. She studied and started training to be a nurse. When she graduated, she joined the army reserve. She stayed busy and never stopped trying to better herself. I imagine this was a lonely time for her. But she never turned her back on herself even though the world around her had done just that, time and time again. She just kept on trucking along.

Sometime during this period she met a fella on the bus

from Hamilton to Toronto and as she told me quite respect-fully, "I was with him." They had a short affair, a fling. Janie was taking contraception but she must have missed a date. She got pregnant . . . again.

Life sped up for her. She isolated herself from the world except for work. Months passed. When she finally saw Bunny again her pregnancy was showing. Bunny knew right away. Bunny was hard as nails when she wanted to be. She saw a preg-nant girl standing in front of her and she turned away. One mistake was enough. No compassion was to be shown for a young girl who obviously needed all the help she could get.

Janie went home that night, packed her bags again and dis-appeared down the lakeshore on a Gray Coach bus to the Big Smoke. She was going to work as a nurse at the Hospital for Sick Children. It was obvious to everyone that she was preg-nant. Everyone except the Sick Kids Hospital, that is. But when they figured it out they let Janie go. Fired. No unmarried pregnant nurses roaming their halls, no way.

So there she was. Stuck in Toronto, pregnant and without a job, money, family or anyone to turn to. She got tossed out of her apartment on Huron Street because she couldn't pay the rent and ended up in a home for lost girls.

It was as if God was with her when she read the newspaper and saw an ad wanting a mother's helper. A nanny position. She travelled up to the north end of the Yonge Street subway line. The Goldbergs let her in, saw the desperate state she was in and gave her the job of taking care of their little boy, Scott. That's all Janie would have to do; for that she could live and eat for free with the Goldbergs, and she would be paid. Janie was saved by the kindness of strangers. She was taking care of a little boy the same age as me. There's always a bit of hell built into the story. The knife was always getting twisted in Janie's back.

Janie delivered her second child at Branson Hospital, and a young Canadian couple adopted the baby girl. I don't know where the couple were from, but they promised to keep the baby in the Toronto area so that Janie could visit her, or at least check in on her. It was a false promise. The couple picked up roots and moved to Trinidad soon after the baby left the hospital. They called the baby Frances. Janie was heartbroken and on her own again.

When Janie told me all this I wondered at the people who had raised me, at the lack of compassion shown to Janie. For some reason it was this story, the story of my sister's birth, that, more than any other, hit me in the chest.

It's funny how the cosmos works. The questions and answers don't always come when we expect them, but they often come at the right time. I had no way of knowing more about my father, but I was visiting my friend Jill Greenwood in San Francisco who told me about a website called 23andMe. She told me I needed to know more about the health of my birth family. Through a DNA swab the site could deliver information about family health history, inherited risk factors and ancestry going way back to Asia and Africa and South America. The cradles of civilization. It seemed like a good idea.

I got home and ordered the DNA kit, and a week later it arrived in the mail. I hate rules and instructions, tax returns and filling out forms of any kind, so I asked Madeline to help. She came over, whipped out the swab, got me to run it around my mouth, filled out the paperwork, stuck the swab back in some plastic bag and mailed it off. An email came three weeks later.

I entered a password, logged in to their site, and there waiting for me was my report.

Among some of the less interesting facts about heart disease and prostate cancer, the report revealed that I may suffer from chronic fatigue syndrome and that my people probably walked out of East Asia many thousands of years ago. It also gave me a list of 644 DNA relatives that were out there—mostly fifth cousins, some seventh cousins—all Native Americans from all over the place, including a few fourth cousins from Kahnawake. Good to know but nothing earth shaking.

Then, months later, out of nowhere I got a message from a woman on the site. Her name was Tracy Howard, which rang no bells, and she lived in Mount Royal.

Her note was simple:

Hello
According to this DNA, Thomas Wilson, you are my grandfather.
　　Please provide me with any facts that you can.
　　How old are you? I am also a Mohawk from Kahnawake but I live in Montreal.

Tracy

It was a mistake of course. I knew I wasn't her grandfather. I wrote back:

Hey Tracy
I am a grandfather myself but I may be a bit young to be yours. I was born in 1959.
　　Hope this helps in some way and good luck with your search . . .

tom

I thought that was that, but then twenty-four hours later Tracy wrote back to me:

Hi Tom,
Yes, you are too young to be my Grandfather.
But I'm still curious, we have over 22% DNA, that would make you a ½ sibling.
Could you be my brother?
I would like to exchange family info, what do you think?
I will start by letting you know, the Mohawk side of me.
My father is Louis Beauvais from Kahnawake, my mother is a beautiful northern European born in Canada.
My father has many children, that is why, maybe you could be my brother.
Hope to hear from you soon.

Tracy

I had been going over and over the revelation of Tracy's note for months and months. I just couldn't bring myself to ask the question I needed to ask. Then one morning I picked Janie up for groceries, and she asked me how my book was coming along. I could have answered with a simple "pretty good" or "not bad." But instead I saw this as the opening I'd been waiting for. "Yeah, Janie. I've hit a wall. You see, your story, and of course I believe your story, is that a man named Rudy West is my father. But I looked up Rudy West online and he's dead. I wouldn't want to drag up any trouble or disturb his family by calling them up, so I only have your recollections to go on.

"Your story is that my father is Rudy West, but my DNA—
and DNA doesn't lie—leads me to a family named Beauvais and
a man named Louis Beauvais. I've been contacted by one of his
daughters. She doesn't know anything about me except that our
DNA matched on a website I went on called 23andMe. I went
on there to find out about health questions I had. And sure
enough, this Beauvais connection was made."

She was quiet as I drove down Charlton Avenue, and I sat
patiently as we whizzed past a couple of blocks. Then she
repeated the name. "Louis Beauvais. . . . Yes. I knew a Louis
Beauvais. . . . In fact, I dated Louis Beauvais a few weeks before
I met your father."

I kept my hands on the wheel, but I started to shake, then
began laughing out loud like an idiot. "You what?" I said. "You
knew him around the same time you knew Rudy West? Janie—
Louis Beauvais is my father." I kept laughing.

Then Janie started to laugh too. "Yes . . . I guess he is."

And that's how simple the truth is for Janie and me.

THOMPSON'S GIFT OF RAIN

I told him to keep it steady down the middle of the lane—no foolin' around, no sudden jerks or stops either—and I finished by looking him straight in the eye and delivering a direct, "You fuckin' fucker."

This was serious business, after all.

He laughed as I leaned forward on the passenger seat, shuffling my ass to the very edge of it, my chest now pressed against the dashboard, unzipping my jeans while taking my cock out and aiming it into the empty Tim Hortons coffee cup. Ahh . . . just in the goddamn nick of time. What a relief. What a luxury. My head cleared, my thoughts lightened, and the pain left my body.

I've been pissing into Tim Hortons cups for forty-one years now. Forty-one years burnin' up and down the road like a tool with my dick in my hand.

Oh sure, I've had plenty of luxury Florida Coach tour buses and the odd private jet and lots of limos, but for the most part it's been eight-cylinder sedans, trailer hitches and white sixteen-passenger extended cabs that make me look more like a guy from a correctional facility than a musician. Forty-one years of trying to get there before the sun goes down, just in time for load-in, sound check and maybe something to eat when we finally hit town.

"Whatta we gonna eat?" The number one question for road survival.

"Do you know a place?"

"Eat yet?"

"No, you?"

The constant chatter that goes on all day. The same old jokes getting the same laughs. Accepting the moment and managing the circumstances, like a travelling Buddha in a twelve-step program. And all the second-hand smoke, coffee and sugar cookies you can handle, man.

"Eat when you can, sleep when you can, and always take the cash."

The great lines that come with the trade.

"Live by the song, die by the road."

Or my bass player Johnny Dymond's timeless beauty, "Well we came a long way, but at least we didn't get paid."

Or the one he uses when he calls his wife after being away for three weeks: "Hi, honey. . . . Is anything okay?"

So here I am in the same spot forty-one years down the road. Balancing myself in the front seat of a van, my face pushed into the windshield like a giant insect on the wrong side of the glass, looking out over Kansas and pissing into a coffee cup and watching the telephone poles flying by, totally satisfied and so uplifted by this moment that I start to sing . . . Jimmy Webb, of course. I mean who else? The song I'm humming, "Wichita Lineman," comes outta these fields.

The sun is going down on the fields. Kansas is exhaling all its October colours and stepping aside for the night to take over. Black-and-white Dorothys and Totos are running down country roads away from home again, and the ghosts of the Clutter family are getting into their pyjamas and kneeling beside their beds to say their prayers, soon to be murdered in cold blood and tossed onto the pile of human horrors inside the pages of Truman Capote's greatest work. For us, the state of Kansas has been a long story that just went on and on like a drunk uncle at a family funeral.

We left the city early enough, but the road beat us to the punchline today. The drive's been torture and we want to keep moving until we reach Denver. We don't want to stop for anything, no way no how. Side-of-the-road toilet breaks are out of the question and the piss cups have been in play. Kansas City the eternal is about five hours behind us. It was hard to leave its candied barbecue and the ghost of Count Basie, his right hand plucking notes between shots of gin, lines of coke and draws of reefer. The city still holds down the rhythm that drags the faithful through the doors of the barrooms and the churches and strokes the heads of schoolchildren and blesses the masses. Saving Southern souls and getting them while they're young.

And on this, my spirit is finally free. After all these years I am feeling stronger than I ever have before.

I never knew my biological father, Louis Beauvais, but by all accounts he was way more of a long-gone daddy than I ever was, and he sure left his own trail of black eyes, broken hearts and bullshit behind him. In the late 1990s, when my addictions were at their worst, when I drove my life into the ditch, I was following the same road my father took forty years before. A man whose ghost crashed through my walls and ruled my own wild spirit when all my soft spots were drowned in whisky and my flesh was weakened by golden-haired witches sitting at the edge of hotel-room beds and the back seats of cars. I never could explain what was happening to me, and I couldn't imagine conjuring up a scapegoat or an excuse for how I was acting. I just didn't know what was wrong with me. I didn't know that I was him.

Fuck the ghosts and fuck the loneliness. There's no excuse for how it all went down.

Now some of the roads I'm on, I'm going down for the first time in my life and I'm going down them with my son, Thompson. He's behind the wheel sturdy as a trucker. He's my soul bandmate, and in many ways the spirit and the guts of this tour. You gotta choose brave warriors to step on stage with every night, and I have the best of the best. He's twenty-four years old and as genuine and soulful a singer as anyone I've ever heard. Every night I look at him on stage and I see the baby I pulled up out of the crib for midnight feedings. I see the open-faced little guy who, along with his sister, Madeline, shaped me into the proud man I have become. He's got a quiet, peaceful strength that carries the load day in and day out as we cut through the middle of the land from sun-up to sundown. The guy is a pro. He figures he was just born in the breed. Together we travel out to the fringes, out to the unknown parts that our quest has created for us.

We drive through the mountains on treacherous roads, like grey ribbons that run around the waist of giant snow-covered beasts, and out across the desert no man's lands. There are a million spirits out there tugging at the steering wheel; they want us to crash and join them for eternity, but Thompson's wits are too sharp and his heart is too pure to be dragged in by their tricks.

Nighttime, lost in America, where we charge out in the darkness past the drunk drivers that killed Johnny Horton and Clarence White. We keep going, feeling the legends of the land all around us, visiting the shrines and looking for the nails that were used to hang our heroes to their crosses. This is the road we read about, and it ends at the Joshua Tree Motor Inn. The holy land.

The Joshua Tree Inn is like getting to drive around in the car that Hank Williams died in, and sure there's some sicko tourist curiosity and shallowness that goes along with the thought of what happened there, but deep down we've known all along that we had to come to the place where we belong.

The silence is like no silence I have experienced in my life. It comes on and rolls over me with a slow, hot breeze that has travelled a thousand miles over three states of desert, collecting the whispers of Indians and the heat of Mother Earth's breath to finally reach me. I light up a smoke, stand up on the roof of the truck and look out over the giant.

The desert embraces me like no other landscape anywhere in the world. I fill my lungs with the burning air, let go, and we drive back to town to our motel. Once we're there we are surrounded by a quiet, peaceful retreat from our usual grind of Holiday Inns and dressing rooms. We eat the remaining weed cookies we bought up in Denver and go swimming in the ancient concrete pool outside our motel room door and take a short walk over the meditation sand and past the erected shrine for Gram Parsons.

Thompson drinks cans of beer and we play guitar in the desert night.

The sky is lit up like a line of poetry.

These are precious moments for sure.

Somewhere out there in wild America we have finally found the peace and love we've always heard about.

THE LONG ROAD HOME

I am flying on the speed of my dreams. Heading down the 401 towards the Quebec border, I am on my way to meet my sisters, Lynn and Tracy, for the first time. The saliva in my mouth is thick like motor oil as I sit in the back seat of the car, nervous, practising my smile in the rear-view mirror.

I am on my way to the mystical land of my missing family. Kahnawake, the patch of land that lies beneath the Mercier Bridge, the home of my mother and father and my ancestors. The land of shape-shifters, corn bread and steak, ironworkers and all the legends that came to life in stories and gossip around our kitchen table when I was a kid.

I stare in the rear-view mirror and slowly, silently mouth the words "I am a Mohawk." I repeat it over and over again like a quiet prayer. Saying it will make it real. A faith I am trying to believe in. The car rolls on.

I am nervous and excited and I have brought the two closest people to me on earth along for the ride. Actually, they are bringing me. I am the guy sitting in the back seat, after all. Thompson is behind the wheel and Madeline is in the passenger seat. These two have stuck by me, pulled me out of the ditch, dusted me off and saved my life with their true loving hearts many times over.

They never lost faith in me. I wrecked the family and they crawled out from the wreckage and hung on tight. Now they're behind the wheel, steering me down the road on the next ride. They are warriors. They are my heart. Because of them I haven't been hardened by this life. I don't have to question who I am. I live every moment with them and for them. They've given me the greatest gift. Awareness.

As we turn off the highway and onto the reserve, the world changes. Not in a way that would impress or shock you. It's not like the trees and the sky change. But inside my chest I can feel the difference, as if I am visiting a life I've lived before. A flash of emotion, a shift in the light and the warmth of home.

The reserve is all around us now. There is no turning back. We drive past the golf course, tobacco stores and stands, craft stores and the graveyard into the heart of the town.

I look out between the front seats, out through the windshield, and a fog I've been in my entire life begins to lift. I know this place. I dreamt myself here as a kid. Dreams that were fantastic. Dreams that took me to times and places that I knew were real.

I'd cruise the Saint Lawrence Seaway and come swooping down these roads on John Lazare's back. My grandfather, sturdy and sure of himself, not a word spoken but I could hear him singing as he carried me. I'd climb off his back and walk through the deepest blues and greens of graveyards and step into the black shadows cast by the great bridge. In my dreams I was safe, surrounded by the ghosts of my ancestors.

Still, I'm a Hamilton guy. I spent Christmases in Kahnawake as a kid and watched lacrosse games on the Six Nations reserve but I haven't really seen how people live on a reserve. I do remember John Lazare. He was an elected chief, an important man, and he lived in a small house and was considered well off. When I was talking on the phone with my half-sister Lynn Beauvais, I had no idea what kind of life she was living. How could I know or assume anything? It was a blind spot in my mirror and that was the problem. For all intents and purposes I am an ignorant white man.

By the time our car pulls into town and hits the centre road, Lynn is on the phone asking where we are, what is taking us so long. She's already bossing me around, acting like an older sister. I tell her we are on the reserve and heading her way. She tells me to look for the old stone building and that she and Tracy will be sitting on the front porch waiting.

Sure enough, as we round the corner and turn up the church road we can see the house. A massive old building that looks like it has been brought back to its original glory from three hundred years ago. Lynn lives there in the beautiful stone heritage building that was built by the French army in about 1735, well before the Mohawks were ushered onto the land surrounding it known as Kahnawake. It has been the centre of government business and acted as a court house and post office, was the only building with a phone, and it acted as a kind of morgue for the thirty-three men who died in the 1907 Quebec bridge disaster. The place looks like it is filled with spirits and time travellers and my sister is running the whole show.

Thompson pulls onto the paved driveway that leads into a three-car garage. We step out of the car and into a rush of mid-afternoon summer heat. Leaving the air-conditioned car is like stepping out of an oxygen tent. Everything slows down to a crawl. I round the corner of the house and walk towards the front porch, and there are Lynn and Tracy. My sisters. I don't know which one is which.

They are both about my age with beautiful round faces and eyes full of life and excitement. "Hey little bro." I recognize the voice from the phone calls. This is Lynn. Her voice is full and direct and has a distinct Kahnawake accent. She stands up out of her chair and greets me. Tracy is smiling bright and wide behind Lynn. She moves to greet me and it almost looks like she is climbing off Lynn's back to do so.

Tracy I know is more soft spoken and she speaks English without an accent. She is almost laughing at the moment. We all are pretty pleased with ourselves, I must say. I introduce Madeline and Thompson. They are bursting with smiles too. This is one happy bunch of Indians, I think.

Lynn leads us inside the house. It is perfect, immaculate. The front double doors open into a grand entrance hall, all ancient wood from thousand-year-old trees. Wood that came from a land that had not been touched by European hands. It looks like a museum. The staircase leading up to the balcony on the second level must be fifteen feet wide.

The ceilings are twenty feet high and everything is manicured and shining bright. I laugh out loud as I follow Lynn across the 250-year-old hardwood floors. I call out behind her, "Hey Lynn, you're like the Zsa Zsa Gabor of Kahnawake."

We all step though the kitchen and out to the back deck. The yard is beautiful. Perfectly landscaped and in the middle is a giant heated salt-water swimming pool. Lynn digs into a cooler and pulls out four beers and a can of Coke for me. We sit around a large round patio table drinking, smoking cigarettes and smiling at one another.

Lynn tells me I look like our dad. My eyes and my brow line are just like his. Then she orders me to show her my feet. All the Beauvais men, it seems, have the same-shaped feet and a bump sticking out of their ankles. I pull my boots off and my socks and put a foot up on the table. "Oh yeah, oh yeah, there it is, that's the Beauvais foot for sure."

When she gets excited her voice rises into spikes of falsetto and her early Flatbush roots come out. She immediately sounds like Marisa Tomei in *My Cousin Vinny*. Lynn does all the talking but Tracy does plenty of quiet investigating from across the table. She smiles the entire time. There's a joy busting out of Tracy.

The conversation slips and dips in and out of Beauvais history. The kids talk about growing up with me and their mom. We all reveal a bit of what we've been up to and missing out on for a lifetime, but we speak as if we've just been away on a weekend getaway, or a short vacation. "Boy is it good to be back home and you'll never guess what happened and who was there etc. etc. . . . ."

Everything is just as normal as can be.

Lynn does say that she wants to keep my visit a secret from her other brothers and sisters—Thea, Leslie, Ann Marie, Chris and Kyle. Louis Beauvais had six kids with his wife. Then there are me and Tracy who've been floating out there in the world. We're all the products of Louis Beauvais's good looks and charming personality. Lynn and the family have proof of me and Tracy through DNA results and the good old Beauvais foot test, but are there others? Nobody knows for sure. Our father may have been a big, handsome, lovable playboy, but that isn't something the family wants to talk about. And they certainly don't want to be confronted with living proof of it. No siree.

Lynn remembers meeting Tracy when they were still little girls. From time to time, Louis would take Lynn along on his dates at the golf course. It may have been on one of those occasions that Tracy's mother, Tracy, Louis and Lynn all came face to face. Apparently when Tracy and Lynn made contact again a few years back and Lynn announced it to her siblings, the news did not go over well.

Lynn wants to keep our visit on the downlow. None of the family is to know anything about it. "Sure thing," I tell her.

Lynn shifts her attention over to Thompson. I can see her staring at the side of his head, squinting like she is looking into the sun. She says out loud, "Oh my god, Thompson, you look just like Tehoriwathe."

Tehoriwathe is the son of my brother Kyle. If there was any doubt concerning me, any lack of faith they may have had in their "foot test," any second thoughts about whether I am in fact their brother, their blood, it's Thompson who wipes all that away.

Now, even though I am meant to be kept under wraps, Lynn just can't control herself. She needs to see Thompson and Tehoriwathe standing side by side. "Who wants pizza?" She gets on the phone and orders up some pie. She sits back down and says, "Let's have some fun." Half an hour later the pizza is delivered by someone who truly could be Thompson's twin, Tehoriwathe. It seems it is not just our feet that we Beauvais men have in common.

From what I can gather, Lynn was very close with our father. "Our Father who art in heaven," Lynn loves to joke. She knows how to dish it out, and she knows how to take it. She is the eldest in the family, and that includes Louis's illegitimate offspring, Tracy and me. The way Lynn talks about our father now, after all these years, there was obviously some blood-on-blood magic that trumped any wrongs they did to each other.

Lynn has the same fondness in her eyes and softness in her voice when she talks about our brothers Christopher and Kyle. The brothers are a couple of lady-killers. Big, strong ironworkers all their lives. Lynn loves to talk about the projects they're working on. It's ironwork talk. It's all about pride and pain and money and the bonding that goes on between workers and families. Lynn speaks the same way generations of women have spoken and the way future generations will speak about the ironworkers.

"Your brother Christopher. He's on a big job in New York. You ought to see what they're working on. It's the same concept as Rockefeller Center. Different buildings, shopping centre, one called the shed," and she angles her hands in front of her and explains that one building goes like this and the other one opens up over the train tracks and the roof opens and the walls lift and it's a performing arts centre. "The cultural shed. The Hudson Yards. It's going to be beautiful. It's a big job. Right down on the Hudson River in Manhattan. And Kyle is working on this thing they call the beehive. The plans for it just came out last week. It's going to be amazing. The centrepiece."

On 9/11, when the World Trade Center came down, my brother Kyle was on the front lines of the rescue and recovery efforts. He was in the first wave of responders to jump into the wreckage looking for survivors and removing remains from what was left of the towers that my uncle Walter and five hundred other Mohawks had built in the sky over Manhattan. Walter had worked ten years on that project, and with great pride had raised the antenna. Kyle walked through Ground Zero, climbing over mountains of twisted iron and steel. The world was on fire, unpredictable, dangerous. He and two hundred Mohawks moved those mountains so the firefighters could get underneath and do their job. Kyle was pulling some wreckage away and came upon a giant piece of steel that he thought was a rocket. It was Uncle Walter's antenna.

When Kyle finally got a break, he went home to Kahnawake. He washed and cleansed himself with tobacco water because parts of all those people who died there were inside his system. He said that the ritual was part of his responsibility to the people who had died there. Those lost souls are carried on by the Mohawk ironworkers.

Most ironworkers who have given up the game and got themselves into the new/old profitable cigarette business still say they miss "the job." They don't miss the travelling but they miss the work. Go ahead and ask one of them, "Do you miss the ironwork?"

The answer comes back a quick, simple and matter-of-fact, "Yup."

There's constant talk around my sister's kitchen about the old days, crimes, characters and misconducts. Sharp minds, spinning wheels, rapid-fire humour, counterpoints, turning corners and bending the truth. The conversation is fantastic. You can drift out of the talk and come back in at any time and still get an earful of action. Small-town chatter. Community talk, everyone knows everybody, this person is related to that person and my cousin and this one and distant relatives and outcasts and arguments back and forth about facts and figures that have packed up, left town and disappeared into the mist over the Saint Lawrence Seaway.

As I walk around the reserve, I come face to face with some of the old-timers who lived and fought through the summer of 1990. It's not easy to get them to share their secrets from the woods and the front lines. Many used to be in Canadian Army Reserve, and some were Vietnam vets. They didn't want to see anyone die and pitied some of those young kids that the army had put in the front lines. For the town of Oka it was all over a goddamn golf course. For the Mohawks it was about plowing over graves and digging up the bones of their ancestors. For the Mohawks, it was about survival. That was the whole Oka Crisis. That's what started it. And the moaning and tears brought on a river of anger, and the anger would bring the SQ (the Quebec provincial police) and the Canadian army and a hatred that had been hidden in plain sight.

The first causality on July 11, 1990, was my nephew Logan, my sister Lynn's little boy. He was riding his bike with no shoes, and Lynn kept yelling out across her front lawn, "Logan, put your bloody shoes on right now!" No sooner had the words left her mouth than Logan's toe slipped through the sprocket and right through the chain. He screamed and looked at his foot and saw that his toe was hanging by a thread of skin.

Lynn ran out and wrapped his foot in a towel. Blood soaked though the towel so fast that she wanted to panic, but she kept her cool. There was no time to call an ambulance, so Lynn's husband, Kenny, put Logan in their car and drove him to the fire station, where they put him in their ambulance and took him to the children's hospital. Three hours later Logan's toe was stitched back on, and Kenny and Logan were in a taxi leaving the hospital.

But the taxi would not go anywhere near the reserve. That day, after weeks of playing cat and mouse with the Mohawk warriors, the army had stationed troops right where the smoke stores were, arming them with shields, batons and rifles. The warriors had cut two-by-fours, lined up and attacked the soldiers, chasing them until they reached the end of the reserve. French mobs had gathered and fires were burning and tempers were ready to burst the Saint Lawrence Seaway wide open. So the taxi left Logan and Kenny at the Mercier Bridge.

The bridge was blocked by the angry French mob. Logan was terrified. He was just three years old, and was so scared that he clung on to his father's neck. Five police officers surrounded the boy and his father, refusing to let the two take the walkway on the Mercier Bridge back home. Kenny moved to step around them, but they blocked his way. Kenny got mad—he was big and tough and didn't give a shit what happened to him. But Logan hung on to his father's neck for dear life. Kenny came to his senses, put his anger aside and turned back.

When he looked towards the river, he saw somebody from the town silently signalling to Kenny like "Get in . . . Get in the boat." They were trying to get people back home and away from the bridge and had seen Kenny and Logan blocked by the mob.

They were dropped two minutes from their house, and as they approached, Lynn ran to meet them. They got into the house safe, where the radio in the kitchen was reporting on the conflict at the bridge. Lynn brought them in and yelled, "Listen, listen!" She turned up the volume, and just then our father, Louis Beauvais, ran up to the kitchen window and said, "They're firing, they're firing on them!" The SQ had lost it.

The impact of the Oka Crisis lived with Logan long after

that summer. Lynn told me that they were in a Chateauguay IGA a couple years later, and Logan was sitting in the front of the cart, dangling his legs. Suddenly, he looked around and began yelling out to the people in the store, "Blockade, blockade! Nobody can pass. Blockade, blockade!" Then he broke down crying. My family were trying to get by, trying to keep their heads down. They were at a disadvantage and had become the enemy whether they were women or children. The stares were still cast and the tension was still thick in the air. The entire community suffered, and even though the roads were getting patched up and the tanks had gone home, the community remained broken for a long time. It was a story I didn't know until the community became mine.

My cousin Carol has arranged for my first visit with Sonny Lazare, and she drives Madeline, Thompson and me the few winding blocks from Lynn's house over to his. Carol drives a huge Cadillac and needs cushions on the driver's seat to see over the steering wheel. Meeting Sonny is one of the reasons I've made the trip back to Kahnawake. It's part of the re-entry. Like finding the Manger or the Titanic or the Ark. My greatest mystery solved, and the evidence right here in front of me. He lives alone now in the house he bought off Joe Delille. Sonny got the house and the adjoining pool hall, settled into the corner lot, ran the business and never left. When I say "alone," I sure don't mean lonely. Sonny has eight kids, 120 grandchildren and great-grandchildren and counting. The house is always busy, and the daughters in particular look out for their father around the clock. His house is the family place.

I don't know if Sonny ever saw me as a little boy. I don't imagine he did. I used to spend Christmases at John Lazare's house, a few blocks away from Sonny's, but I was never allowed off the property in case someone recognized me. I was just another big-headed boy, but in Kahnawake I was suspect, a pale Mohawk stranger that my family feared would start talk around town.

Sonny's front door is the end of my long walk home. A walk I didn't know I was going to be making. I never knew where I belonged, and as a result I went through life with a question mark above my head. When you're not sure who you are or where you came from, life is a little more difficult. You're aware of everyone around you. You're always the outsider. You keep your fists clenched in your pockets in case the world challenges you or looks at you the wrong way.

The unknown led me down twisted paths, and I found plenty of trouble there. I'd lie awake wondering, and then feel guilty for wondering. I was constantly spinning, looking for ways to calm myself, to slow myself down, always searching for answers that were not out there. I looked for ways to prove I was alive, that I was real, that I belonged. I used sex to be in the here and now, and booze and drugs to wipe everything out again. It was a deadly circle of abuse that I kept going for decades. But I didn't have to be on this crooked path. It could have been easier.

I thought about all of this as I knocked on Sonny Lazare's door for the first time. Standing there at the door, I pictured Bunny and George and 162 East 36th Street and Janie and the Hamilton streets I grew up on and all my French and Irish relatives who knew my story and never told me. But everything, the thoughts and regrets and questions about life and who I was, disappear into smoke as the door opens and my cousin Sharon appears in the doorway, smiling. Behind her is Sonny, sitting in his easy chair. He pulls himself out of his chair, tears in his eyes, arms outstretched. I've never had this kind of welcome from a family member before. "You were supposed to be raised here where you belong. You are a Mohawk."

I am the son he was not allowed. He accepts what happened, but still hints that I was taken from him. I was supposed to be his. He was well on his way to filling his house with kids, and his wife, Hazel, agreed that they would raise me. Then she found out that she too was pregnant, with my cousin Sharon, and John Lazare made his trip to scoop me up into his back seat and take me home, but instead came back to Kahnawake empty handed. Bunny and George made a home for me in Hamilton, and that was that.

He's waited fifty-six years for this moment and is an old man now. So am I. But I'm here. I'm scared and scarred but I've survived. I'm alive and lucky as hell.

A FIGHTING CHANCE

A few years ago Janie sent several Tupperware storage containers over to my house with my housekeeper, who I also hire to keep Janie's apartment in order for her. She called to tell me they were coming and that they were full of Bunny and George's old belongings. Things from a lifetime ago. Things they had held on to until the end. I sometimes hate those kinds of things, the ones that meant everything to the departed but nothing in the land of the living. In antique stores and flea markets, I'm always saddened to find the cherished possessions of an old woman—a picture of her dog, salt and pepper shakers, dishes, crafts—a constellation of lost memories thrown onto a table for people to rummage through. I'm sensitive about this shit, and so until very recently I had been unable to lift the lid off the containers full of Bunny and George, or maybe I just knew that I was inside there too.

I was ready. I reached inside one container and found George's Air Force medals and his formal dress uniform. Fifty-two years before, I'd bundled this stuff up and brought it to my grade one class bursting with pride to show off my war hero's honours. I reached into another and found Bunny's old coin collection. I remembered her sorting through these coins in the evenings, after she'd finished the dishes, at the kitchen table back on 36th Street. She'd check the dates, record the details of each coin on a small cardboard frame and then place the coin at the frame's centre and staple it into its presentable resting place. I held one tight in my fist trying to feel Bunny somewhere inside there.

As I went through the containers marked Bunny and George my breath became heavy and I was hit by the same claustrophobic feeling that came over me when Bunny died. I pictured myself in one of those old black-and-white movies. I was the boxer hitting the mat after the knockout punch, the air temporarily drained out of him. The cards of my life shuffled into order and exposed right there in front of me. I closed my eyes as my mind raced through memories. I thought about the day Thompson was born. How amazed I was with every bit of him. How scared I was for Madeline. How protective I felt of her. I remembered we were driving down King Street into Westdale heading back to the McMaster University hospital. Back to Sandy and the new baby. I looked down at Madeline playing in the front seat with a Barbie I had just bought her. We were alive and electric and we were alone in the world together at that moment. She looked up at me smiling. I was a father whole, connected. I remember all this like it happened twenty minutes ago. Greg Keelor came on the radio singing "Lost Together," and I broke. I knew how deeply and completely my kids were inside me and think that's the feeling I missed from Bunny and George. That's what I missed from Janie. But I had it all delivered to me in kings and aces with my own kids.

I've lived in uncertainty most of my life. Running from myself. Running from Bunny and George who gave me everything they had but in the end it wasn't enough and it wasn't their fault. Then my happiest childhood memories pushed themselves forward. I remembered being danced around the living room in Bunny and George's arms to "Till We Meet Again" at the end of *Don Messer's Jubilee,* and running back and forth in my playpen in the front foyer of the house while Bunny cooked something up on the stove and George sat at at the kitchen table. I thought about how George, even though he was blind, would come to my hockey games at Inch Park and stand in the corner holding Bunny's arm, smoking Export Plains and listening to the skates and sticks of the peewees and the other parents screaming and cheering their kids on, and how I would skate by that corner and say, "Hi, Dad, it's me," so he knew it was my shift. That one memory flash, that one card flipping through the deck, was what opened my heart to Bunny and George. Broke it wide open, in fact. They gave me a fighting chance and you can't ask for more than that. The cards flipped by, and I felt like I knew everything there was to know, and I felt like I knew nothing.

ACKNOWLEDGEMENTS

Oh the love . . .

That I've received.

It's come to me like arrows shot far and wide from hearts vast with love. I'm like the guy riding into town half dead, dirty, with feathers and handfuls of arrows sticking out of my hat. I've been taken in by lovers who have brought me back to life.

My reasons to be thankful come and go from Hamilton to Halifax to Toronto to Limerick and back. From David Wiffen to Frankie Venom to Miles Davis, the Cowboy Junkies, Charles Bukowski, Michael Ondaatje and Henry Miller. *The Wizard Oz* and *The Heart is a Lonely Hunter*.

I've been shaped by beautiful minds.

I've been inspired and I've written countless songs just by tuning in and listening to Bob Dylan singing "Things Have Changed" or Tom Waits "Goin' Out West." Songs that dragged out the poet in me and opened the doors of possibility.

Muddy Waters' *Folk Singer* and Miles Davis's *Kind of Blue* are still the greatest recordings of all time.

The life I've lived seems so small and fast so far but in reality what I've been given from family and friends, fellow artists and associates is so great and has propped me up and kept me going through the years and the tears, the questions and faith and vomit and gasoline.

I thank them for this opportunity. I came from nowhere and I'll go back there one day.

This book is for my family.

Madeline and Thompson. I'm so proud, so thankful, to have you guys in my life every day. You are my heart. You've made me work hard to be a better man.

Janie, Bunny and George, these people have given me a fighting chance, truly.

My hometown Hamilton, Ontario, has inspired me from the moment it clocked me in the jaw. I keep writing about Hamilton and Hamilton keeps ignoring my words. It's a tough audience and a mean-spirited critic that constantly sends me out to the woodshed where I dust myself off and try again to get it right.

Madeline and Thompson's mother, Sandy, taught me what a family is. She tried her best with me but in the end I was just a hard dog to keep on the porch. We go through periods of silence and separation but we always come back to the dinner table with the people we made and love.

My grandsons Hawksley and Levon. You guys are still young

and are already challenging the world around you. I hope I'm still here thirty years from now to see the beautiful wild men I know you'll become. And hey, Jesse Dore, you are an inspiring family man. Thanks for that, buddy.

My beautiful family in Kahnawake. Lynn and Tracy, thank you for opening the door for me.

I met Margot Burnell the week I started writing this book. She made falling in love so easy and she made it easy for me to fall in love with her. Her pure and honest heart has guided me through what I consider dangerous doorways and I've done it without fear, maybe for the first time in my life. Forward we go, Margot.

Ray Farrugia is my oldest and closest friend, the godfather to my children and my musical partner for the last thirty-five years. He's seen me through some of my darkest hours and celebrated and cheered me on throughout my life. I could never imagine going through this without you, Ray. Same with Colin Cripps. There's a complicated guy who leads with his heart every time, and lucky for me, he's taken the lead for me many times.

Dave Bidini called me one day and asked me if I'd ever thought about writing a book. I think I said, "Fuck no. That sounds like too much work." Thanks, Dave, for dragging me off the elevator and into the boardroom at Doubleday/Penguin Random House.

Scott Sellers for his positive and upbeat energy.

Martha Kanya-Forstner edited this book. That is of course too simple a description of her involvement. Martha became my trusted confidante who kept my heart on the pages and the story speeding straight down the road. Martha, you are a masterful creative partner and a loving friend. Thanks for the ride. And thanks too to Ward Hawkes.

I spent hours upon hours lying in bed with Cathy Jones entertaining her with stories about my childhood. She would shake the bedroom walls with laughter. She was always a fantastic audience for me and I indulged myself in her unguarded responses. Shocked or near tears, she helped me to start believing in who I really am. Cathy was stunned by my unconventional upbringing and was the first person to tell me that I should write a book or a movie or something, anything.

My friend, writer Ryan Knighton searched me out on the streets of East Vancouver after a show. He was the first fan to tell me I should write down some of my stories and stage banter. He started the wheels turning. He handed me his book *Cockeyed* and it further inspired me and made the task of writing easier to accept.

My agent, Jack Ross, told me to write a book three years ago. Jack was blunt, unemotional when he said told me this but he certainly tossed me on the road I find myself travelling today.

Aaron Goldstein patiently listened to my stories on stage for the last nine years and inspired me to keep on talking and talking and talking.

My long-suffering manager, Allen Moy, and Madeline Wilson took me out to dinner three years ago and cornered me with the idea of writing a book. Allen always believed in me and I thank him for never falling off the bull when it came to me. A week after our dinner, out of nowhere Doubleday called me into a meeting to discuss the possibility of having me as one of their authors. That's some fantastic mojo we put out into the universe that night, Allen and Mad.

The people who Hanna Clayton, Jayne Scala, Grace and Aaron Goldstein sat with me in my office and lovingly listened to me talk and transcribed my ideas.

Thanks to: Ken Peters, Mark Stringer, Larry Myers, Mark Rogers, the late Doug Crawford, the late Scott Pollock, Stewart Pollock, Nina Honda, Dave Cross, the Walker family of East 36th Street, the East Mountain, Andrea Ramalo, Jesse O'Brian, Mimi Shaw, Ed Clayton, Edward Shaw, Penny Shaw, Grace Williams, Ann Marie Rousseau, Abby Kanak, Steve McDuffee, Ralph Nicole, Alison Liss, Sherelle Wilsack, Lisa Wilsack, Eddie Kopas, Brent Titcomb and his fantastic four family, Bruce Cameron, Bill Powell, Jason Avery, Carl Keesee, Greg Cannon, Dave Rave, Tim Gibbons, Rick Andrew, Mike Roth, Yvonne Matsell, Barb Sedun, Gary Furniss, Dave Quilico, Mishelle Pack, Janet Baker, Rick Camilleri, Alison Brock, Mary Mill, Don Oates, Sandy Power, Malcolm Burn, Denise Donlon, Murray McLauchlan, Ralph James, Stefanie Purificati, Bob Lanois, Jocelyne Lanois, Dan Lanois, Dennis Drere, Bob Nickling, Tracey Weber, Ken Ashcroft, Bernie Finklestein, Colin Linden, Janice Powers, Stephen Fearing, John and Denise Dymond, Gary Craig, Michael Timmins, Betty and Jim Fyshe, Suzy Miller, Chris Mak, Teenage Head, the spirit of Frankie Venom, Celia Arruda, Michael Merryman Murphy, Russell Wilson, Charlie Ferguson, Ted Hoyle and the ever tenacious spirit of the great Dan Achen.

I have unchained all the prisoners from my basement and freed the ghosts from my attic.

I was the guy who ended up holding the keys to their freedom. It was me who let them out.

It's a job that no one else could do and one that comes with great consequence because those ghosts and prisoners are standing around me now all day, all night long.

I told my truth the way I heard it and the way I remembered it and that's all I have.

Everything else is bullshit.